"Every once in a while a book comes along that is life-changing. *Like Father, Like Son* is that kind of book and it's that in spades. Pete Alwinson has given us a gift of profound biblical insight and he's done it with clarity, humor, and freshness. If you're a man, you'll 'rise up' and call Pete blessed. If you're a woman, you will too . . . because you'll understand about men and also about your heavenly Father. Give this book to everybody you know. They will thank you."

Steve Brown, Key Life radio broadcaster; professor (emeritus), Reformed Theological Seminary, Orlando

"If ever a book deserved to become a bestseller it's the uplifting, winsome, and tightly written *Like Father, Like Son*. An ineffable feeling that I'm going to be okay swept over me as I read this book. I hope you will experience it too. You'll never read anyone who has a better grasp of the gospel of God's grace than Pete Alwinson. The result? He doesn't write to beat you up, but set you free."

Patrick Morley, Author; Bible teacher; founder, Man in the Mirror

"Imagine this. The God who created all things, visible and invisible, becomes the spiritual Father of everyone who believes in Jesus. Nothing is more reassuring and invigorating than experiencing how this is true. Pete Alwinson speaks from this experience. He knows God as his Father and he has charted a course for others to follow as they seek to live in the love of the Father as well. You want to read this book."

Richard L. Pratt, Jr., President, Third Millennium Ministries

"We guys struggle with what gnaws at us on the inside, what creates that edge, that fear of not measuring up. This book answers that question and shows us the answer to being who we were meant to be. Pete's book is crucial to our journey to be men. He illuminates our identity, our value, and our freedom by calling us into grace—a real relationship with our perfect Father."

Jeff Kemp, Former NFL QB; VP at FamilyLife; author of *Facing the Blitz*

"Pete Alwinson is onto something huge. The disquiet, the uncertainty, the insecurity that all men feel can be traced to an emptiness that only the Father can fill. In the pages of this book, we meet the Father again."

Nate Larkin, Founder of the Samson Society; author of *Samson and the Pirate Monks: Calling Men to Authentic Brotherhood*

"Although some fathers are distant or abusive, my father was not. He loved me and I knew it because he said it and he showed it. As a result I wanted to honor my father and not disappoint him, even though I knew whatever I did would never change his love for me. It was natural, therefore, for me to relate to my Heavenly Father the same way. God loves me eternally in Christ and I know that. As a result of his amazing grace, I desire to honor and obey him. Read this book to understand more about the motivating and freeing love of a good father, whether an earthly father or your Heavenly Father."

Robert C. (Ric) Cannada, Jr., Chancellor Emeritus, Reformed Theological Seminary

"Most men remember their fathers with a mixture of both fondness and disappointment. We could use help in constructing a healthy way to deal with both our past and our future, not just for ourselves but to better love those in our lives now. Dr. Alwinson gives us the spiritual and emotional empowerment to love others the way our heavenly Father has loved us."

Joel C. Hunter, Senior Pastor, Northland, A Church Distributed

"Pete knows what makes a man a man; first because he's a man who is tough and tender. He also has wisdom from working with men, but most importantly he directs us to the True Man, Jesus Christ. This book is a compelling and healing message of the power of the Father in making men that we will recommend to all our clients and partners."

Tom Wood, President, CMM, Inc.; coauthor of *Gospel Coach*

"This is the book I wish I had written on fatherhood. No guilt, lots of encouragement, and appropriate challenges."
Larry Kreider, Founder, Gathering of Men, US; author

"In the high-stakes, high-performance, success-driven system that is American culture today, it seems that most men have one feeling in common: they don't measure up. The insecurities of men run deep because their identity is almost wholly performance based. For that reason, I believe *Like Father, Like Son* is a refreshing reminder men are desperate to hear. Pete Alwinson does a masterful job of connecting a man's identity to the fundamental nature of our heavenly Father, bathing the reader in the healing balm of God's grace. When a man reads this book, I think he will see himself with new, Christ-like eyes, he will hold his head up a little taller, and he will be more equipped to love and serve because he will be doing so out of a cup that is now full—the cup of God's gracious love."
David D. Swanson,
Senior Pastor, First Presbyterian Church of Orlando; author of *Everlasting Life: How God Answers Our Questions about Grief, Loss, and the Promise of Heaven*

"Pete Alwinson is onto something! The father wound runs deep in men leaving them ill-equipped for parenting, and their children are languishing for lack of father affirmation and engagement. As men are re-parented, however, by the Father love of God, old wounds are healed and grace is received to give their children. *Like Father, Like Son* is the right prescription for healing our culture's deepest wounds and unleashing dads to give the father love their kids crave."
Ray Cortese, Pastor, Seven Rivers Presbyterian Church

"In father and son relationships, there is always the good, the bad, and the ugly. What I so appreciate about *Like Father, Like Son* is the redemptive message without regard to one's earthly father or circumstances. Here's a formative and transformative book for men to live into authentic victory and to be on-purpose."
Kevin W. McCarthy, Author, *The On-Purpose Person*

"If you're a man—read this book. If you're a son—read this book. If you have a son and you want him to be a man—read this book. Pete has captured the essence of real manhood and how it flows from a man's relationship with his heavenly Father."

Bill Perkins, Best-selling author; speaker;
founder, Million Mighty Men

"Like a good father, Pete gives men permission to examine their sorrows, to understand why guys are the way we are, and to emerge from our isolation, strong and true, into the community of light and life."

Wes Yoder, Author of *Bond of Brothers*

"I've become exhausted by the many how-to books on being a man or fathering. Pete's new book, *Like Father, Like Son,* is a refreshing challenge to parent BY GRACE and swim in adventurous freedom. Such gospel-centric parenting is not only energizing for dads, but also able to captivate the hearts of young men. Pete's creative ideas and engaging stories are tried and proven. I should know. Pete's adult son, Jon, is an active, vibrant husband and leader in the church I help lead."

Alan Scott, Lead Pastor, Cumberland Community
Church, Atlanta, Georgia

"In Psalms 32:8, the LORD says, 'I will guide you along the best pathway for your life. I will advise you and watch over you.' In this book, *Like Father, Like Son,* Pete Alwinson has written how the fatherhood of God plays this out in the context of a man's life. The relationship that God desires with each of us is the same as God desires for each man to have with his son or daughter. This is an encouraging book for every man of God and his desire to make a difference in the lives of his sons and daughters."

Darrel Billups, Executive Director,
National Coalition of Ministries to Men

"What is a 'real man'? With definitions hurled at us through every medium, where should we turn? Culturally, the idea of 'father' and 'son' have many connotations, which have a profound impact on how a man relates to God. Why then have men been burdened with behavior modification, generalized rules of what constitutes a 'real man'? *Like Father, Like Son* replaces the checklists with God's grace. By exploring men's biblical identity as sons of the Father, Pete Alwinson unpacks the greatest news proclaimed, the gospel. And the gospel changes everything about what it means to be a 'real man'!"

Bobby Raulerson, Grace Church
Pastor, Oviedo Campus, Florida

"Like Father, Like Son is different from any book I have read in my own journey to become a better man and follower of Christ. It starts at the foundation of understanding the depths of God's love for man. It's not a self-help manual or quickstep guide; it truly begins to transform your heart into a new way of living under the grace and love of God."

Mitch Todd, Senior Pastor – River Run Church

"For a father or son, Pete Alwinson encourages us to first know our heavenly Father, so our earthly father-son relationship will thrive. What a guide he has provided for dads to be godly fathers. And driving home the point that it is never, never too late to connect with God or our son(s)."

Jay Crouse, Founder, Men and the Church

LIKE FATHER, LIKE SON

LIKE FATHER, LIKE SON

How Knowing God as Father Changes Men

Pete Alwinson

New
Growth
Press

www.newgrowthpress.com

New Growth Press, Greensboro, NC 27404
Copyright © 2015 by Key Life

Cover Design: Faceout Books, faceoutstudio.com
Interior Design and Typesetting: Lisa Parnell, lparnell.com

ISBN 978-1-942572-04-6 (Print)
ISBN 978-1-942572-05-3 (eBook)

Library of Congress Cataloging-in-Publication Data
Alwinson, Pete.
 Like father, like son : how knowing God as father changes
men / Pete Alwinson.
   pages cm
 ISBN 978-1-942572-04-6 (print) — ISBN 978-1-942572-
05-3 (ebook)
1. God (Christianity)—Fatherhood. 2. Christian men—
Religious life. 3. Men (Christian theology) I. Title.
BT153.F3A49 2015
248.8'42—dc23
                                        2015027046

Printed in United States of America

22 21 20 19 18 17 16 15   1 2 3 4 5

Contents

To Those
Who Have Shaped Me
by Grace . . .

The Father who, because of Jesus and by his Spirit, said he would never leave me nor forsake me, and has always been true to his word.

My wife Caron, whose love, faithfulness, and wisdom for me, our family, church, and friends are a warm and constant reminder of undeserved favor.

Our children Joel, Jon, and Jessie Alwinson, and our incredible daughters-in-law Aly and Sandra Alwinson, and granddaughters Maggie and Molly Alwinson, who fill me with joy and give me more love and support than I deserve.

Steve Brown, my beloved mentor for more than thirty years (that long?!), who accepted me unconditionally as a young and raw pastor (and man). He modeled and poured grace into me sacrificially, and he was loyally unafraid to have my name associated with his. Never wanting to be a guru, Steve has taught me more about grace, the gospel, and God the Father than any other human being. I owe him more than I will ever know.

George Bingham and the staff at Key Life Network, Inc., who have encouraged my every step and who live radical grace with me every day.

The church family of Willow Creek Presbyterian Church, who welcomed the gospel of grace and taught me grace for more than twenty-five years.

Pat Morley, Brett Clemmer, David Delk, and the team at Man in the Mirror, who understand and serve men more any other team I know.

The guys at Key Life Men who "get it" that grace builds men and drink it in gladly each week, impacting their families, community, and churches in powerful ways.

And thank you to Barbara Miller Juliani, an incredibly intelligent, experienced, wise, kind, and encouraging editor who made a first-time author's words worth reading, along with all the tremendous staff at New Growth Press!

Introduction

"Tell me about your relationship with your father." I've said this to countless men over the years because I've found it cuts to the heart of a man's identity. The response usually tells me it is a tough subject. Many guys will pause, look down, and struggle to describe a subject that they probably wished I hadn't brought up. Then I often hear some variation of, "It's complicated. It's a long story."

Yes, it is. For many men the very word "father" or "dad" can elicit a wide range of emotions: fear, rejection, loss, guilt, anger/rage, anxiety, and ambivalence. Sometimes they just shake their heads as if to say, "I don't get him. I have more questions than answers about him and about our relationship."

Guys who have a great earthly father have no problem with the dad question and usually fire back something like, "My dad was always there for me. He came to my games. We did stuff together. I knew he loved me." Those men often have a confidence, security, and strength that other guys pick up on, but cannot quite decipher. *What is it about that guy that is different?* we wonder. Often the most pronounced difference in these men is the positive influence their fathers played in their lives.

Fathers play a key role in the formation of all their children, but there is something unique about the way this plays out with their sons. A boy learns (or doesn't learn) to be a man primarily from the most significant man in his life. If that man—his father or father-figure—is absent, abusive, or disengaged, that will shape the kind of man a boy becomes, whether by molding himself in that image or by battling against it.

This is not to say that mothers are not key influences on their children as well. But too often moms are expected to raise children on their own—without help from the men who fathered those children. The result is children left adrift—especially boys, who are trying to find their way in an increasingly complicated world without a man to guide them.

My deep conviction is that as the men go, so goes the culture. A culture stands or falls on the quality of its men. The same holds for the church: as the men of the church go, so goes the church. A man's role is so crucial in all spheres of life that from the first man Adam to today, their actions—both good and bad—have profoundly shaped the course of history. And fathers play a central role in shaping boys into men who know how to use their strengths, talents, and gifts to love well, care for those who are weaker, and become faithful husbands and fathers.

Perhaps that rings true for you—you do feel adrift without the love and guidance of a father. The good news is that when a man becomes a Christ-follower, he gains a father—and not just any father, *the* Father. Even men who've experienced a wonderful earthly dad need a relationship with their heavenly Father for the simple reason that all dads are finite, imperfect, and temporary. God the Father makes all the difference in a man's life and in the lives of all around him. Why? Because like Father, like son.

God the Father builds sons who come to grips with their core identity as *his sons* and develops his character in them to thrive in their various roles in life. When men thrive and flourish, they become the sons, husbands, fathers, brothers, and friends that encourage others to grow and flourish. Our world desperately needs more men like that.

I hope you'll join me in the adventure that follows in this book as we see how God as Father creates, nurtures, provides, protects, bestows identity, sets free, leads the way in adventure, guides, provides wisdom, and gives daily grace to his sons. It all starts with knowing the love of your heavenly Father. That's what makes all the difference. Like Father, like son.

Like most adventures, you will want to gather some companions for your journey. Please consider going through this book with a small group of fellow adventurers—guys who also want to spend time thinking through what it means to know their heavenly Father's unfailing love and learn to live out of that love. I've included questions at the end of each chapter that can be used to go deeper into the truths presented in that chapter.

A note to women: If you are reading this book, please don't take the focus on men as sons to mean that women are not also dearly loved daughters of the living God. Although I am choosing to focus on men and their relationship with their heavenly Father, all that I say about identity equally applies to women. This book is simply focused on how the fatherhood of God plays out in the context of a man's life. I hope it encourages you and the men in your life!

1

The Irreplaceable Father

"I believe in God the Father, Almighty,
Maker of Heaven and Earth."
Apostles' Creed

"I find my father everywhere—in the mirror,
of course, in the cupid's bow of my four-year-old son's
lips, in the tugging of my heart toward rage even as
my hair goes white, and in the hate and hurt whetted
in my family's soul. I find my father because I want
to find him, because I grew up without him, starving
for him, because I'm still greedy to redeem our love."[1]
Scott Raab

Ask any man about the importance of his father to him
and you will get a story—some positive and some more
negative—that confirms his father's significance in his
life. Talk to some guys in prison, as I have, and you will
get specifics from men who trace their life's missteps to
being unfathered, underfathered, or rejecting their father's counsel. On the opposite track are the stories from
guys who have had a great earthly father train them and
point their way into manhood. When you think about

the role of a father in the life of his children, there's an inherent logic to the reality that dads are critical. *Of course, we think, the most dominant man in the home, maybe the only other man in the home, is going to significantly impact the young boys in the home. That just makes sense.*

Men hunger for a great relationship with their fathers. The lack of that relationship marks their lives and affects all their other relationships. And, sadly, many men today are trying to make their way through life without the help, guidance, and love of their father. Too many men are marked by what some have called the "father wound,"[2] and stronger still, "the absent-father neurosis."[3]

How does it affect a boy when his father is absent, abusive, uninvolved, or just plain uncaring? Here is a sample from what many men have shared with me about the impact a difficult relationship with their dad had on their life:

> "When I became a teenager, my father's relationship with me became very difficult and essentially came to an unofficial, functional close. It was as if he could no longer relate to me. It seemed that there was a sudden disconnect, like he could not understand me. By ninth grade, I was empty and distant. I couldn't cry. It was that year that I started cutting and made plans for suicide."
>
> "If I am perfect, then my dad won't criticize me."

"It was during my late elementary and middle school years that I began to understand that my father was an alcoholic. The end result was fatherless teenage years, and really a mostly fatherless adulthood. I grew more and more distant from my dad simply because he was unable to relate to me at any level."

"My father died, so the only father figure I had was my father-in-law. He often said that I wasn't really a man because I was not a millionaire."

"I remember running after my dad when he was pulling out of the driveway—trying to catch him so I could spend time with him. He just kept driving. I knew that I was an inconvenience to him."

"From the very beginning my 'dad' (an uncle who was taking care of my brothers and me) sexually abused all three of us. We would do devotions in the morning, and he would abuse us at night."

Sadly, those are just a few of the unsettling things men have shared with me about their fathers. As a pastor who is committed to developing men, the importance of the father in a boy's life has been affirmed again and again in talking with men from all kinds of backgrounds, but amazingly the role of fathers is a relatively *new* area of psychological and sociological study.

Clinical psychologist Ditta Oliker points to family structural changes at the beginning of the twentieth century that resulted in the sidelining of fatherly influence in children's lives and the redefinition of a man's worth.[4] Increasingly, a man was defined by how well he provided for his family. As the field of psychology developed, research on the healthy development of children focused on the moms, who were the primary caregivers. Dads, if mentioned in the studies at all, were in the category of "other influences." But for the past thirty to forty years, more and more studies have been conducted that show the critical importance of fathers. As one researcher put it, "Fathers are far more than just 'second adults' in the home. Involved fathers bring positive benefits to their children that no other person is as likely to bring."[5]

Although the social sciences might be just catching on to the importance of fathers, in the Bible God always affirmed the key and central leadership role that a father has in his family. God gave Adam, the first human father, the lead in naming the animals and caring for creation (Genesis 2:15–20). God called Adam and Eve to partner in the job of being fruitful and multiplying (Genesis 2:23–24). Dads and moms are not supposed to go it alone. God designed families to function with a dad and mom working together with the mutual love and respect that forms the foundation for a healthy family. And in the context of mutual love, God calls fathers to be the spiritual leader in their home (Ephesians 5:22–6:4).

The Difference Your Heavenly Father Makes

So fathers are important! Of course you probably already know that and you might be wondering *what now?* If you didn't have a good relationship with your earthly father (and no father-son relationship is perfect), are you doomed to figure life out on your own or, even worse, repeat the same mistakes you saw in your father?

Well, here's the good news—you have a perfect heavenly Father! It makes all the difference in the world when you realize that God is *your* father, the most important father in *your* life. God *the* Father and God *as* Father is the truly irreplaceable Father. When we start relating to God as Father, it's absolutely amazing how it transforms us and changes our lives for the better. That's the bottom-line thesis of this book.

I'm not saying that you should minimize the impact your earthly father has made in your life. I believe that a man has to come to terms with the reality of what it was like being his father's son, and how their relationship has shaped, guided, and possibly wounded him as a man. Like many men, I've had to grieve a distant, abusive, and uninvolved father. As a young man, I was adrift—trying to figure out what it meant to be a man on my own. What has made all the difference in the world to me is knowing that God is my irreplaceable heavenly Father.

Even though I couldn't fix my relationship with my dad, God the Father stepped in. When I became a Christ follower, I found that I was no longer a nameless street boy abandoned by his preoccupied, demanding, and unhappy father. I was an individually valued son—known and specially loved before the foundation of the world by the only One of ultimate status (Romans 8:28–29). My value to the Father was proven by Jesus's rescue of me on the cross (John 6:37; 10:14–15). As I became convinced of God's love for me despite what I really deserved, the Spirit of God drew me into a relationship with the Father that will never end (John 3:5–8).

I am still shocked that I'm not an interruption or an inconvenience to my heavenly Father. Growing up with a father who always seemed angry at me (Why? What did I do?), I was stunned to realize that my Father in heaven wasn't angry at me. All his anger had already been poured out on Jesus. No longer was I alone in a hard world trying to figure everything out on my own (Hebrews 13:5). Now I had a completely available Father who wanted to and was determined to develop this rough boy into a man. Grief over the abandonment of my earthly father gave way to joy because of the Father's never-ending attention and love. Because I have a Father through Jesus, I have power to live in this crazy world through all the stages of my life (Philippians 2:12–13). I'm changed and changing because I am loved forever by my Father in heaven.

Created for Relationship

We were made for a close father-son relationship with God. Do you remember how things started between God and Adam? The all-powerful God spoke the world into existence, making something beautiful out of nothing at all. Finally, the pinnacle of his creation was Adam and Eve. He made his son Adam in his own image and literally breathed life into him. The two walked together in the garden every day. God spoke with Adam, explaining his purpose and responsibilities (Genesis 1:26–2:7).

In the creation account, God the Father gives his sons (and his daughters too) the identity that is foundational for a confident and bold life. Genesis 1 and 2 teaches us that we are not cosmic surprises, anomalies, or mistakes, but that we are the intentional creations of a personal God. Unlike the rest of creation, we are made in God's image, exhibiting intellect, emotions, and will, just like God. God made people in his image so he could have a unique and personal relationship with us.

A man's *core identity* is that he is a special creation of God, an image-bearer, and more relationally, a son of God. The word *son*, when spoken with warmth and dignity by a loving Father, strikes a deep chord of joy in a man, confirming his worth. You are a son of the living God because your Creator-Father made you in his image so he could have a close Father-son relationship with you.

A Ruined Relationship

You probably already know that Adam's relationship as God's son was too quickly ruined. When Adam and Eve were tempted to distrust God's love for them and to believe the words "you will be like God," they turned away from God to go their own way and ushered in all of the brokenness we live with today. Instead of a close relationship with God and each other that would last forever, Adam and Eve were sent from the garden.

Away from God's presence, they would struggle in their relationship with each other. Adam's work became hard, and in the end death would come to both (Genesis 3:14–19). God created men to be his sons—to image him by using their strength to protect and care for all he made—yet in one short generation men's nature turns violent as one son kills another out of jealousy and rage (Genesis 4:1–8).

All of our difficulties with our earthly fathers and our struggle to know our identity and purpose are inherited from our first father, Adam. All men (and women, but we are focusing on men here) have followed in Adam's footsteps—going their own way instead of God's way and suffering the loss of their identity as sons of the living God. Your struggles with your earthly father, your struggles to know who you are as a man, your struggles in relationships, your fears, your anger—they are all inherited from Adam, your first father.

Relationship Restored

Going your own way, what the Bible calls "sin," has radically distorted our nature and made it impossible for us to experience the fatherhood of God. But even as God was telling Adam and Eve about the destruction their sin caused, he held out the hope of a savior. There would be a son who would crush Satan (Genesis 3:15). A man would arrive on the scene who would do what Adam failed to do. His name is Jesus, and he is the perfect son. He always did his Father's will. He always loved his heavenly Father and the people around him. God calls him his "beloved Son, with whom I am well pleased" (Matthew 3:17).

This perfect son would set in motion the Father's plan to restore relationship with his children. Jesus's perfect life and willing death on the cross for the sins of his people destroyed death forever. The resurrection—God's amen to Jesus's work on the cross—has begun a whole new era. Jesus accomplished in his death, burial, and resurrection what we could never achieve: restoration of our relationship as sons with the Father. "But when the fullness of time had come, God sent forth his Son, born of woman, born under the law, to redeem those who were under the law, so that we might receive adoption as sons. And because you are sons, God has sent the Spirit of his Son into our hearts, crying, 'Abba! Father!' So you are no longer a slave, but a son, and if a son, then an heir through God" (Galatians 4:4–7).

Your adoption as sons is by grace, freely available to all who turn to Jesus and accept his sacrifice by faith. No performance on your part, no great success, no failure, no damning words from other people, can ever change who you are: a son. In Christ your identity as a son of the living God is restored. Your *core identity*—that which will never change throughout every phase and season of life—is that you are a special creation of God, an image-bearer, and a son of God.

Because of Jesus all that was twisted and broken in the fall is being restored and redeemed. Your relationship with your heavenly Father is restored when you go to Jesus and ask for forgiveness for your many sins. In him, your relationship with your heavenly Father is remade. In Christ, the Father's words to Jesus also become his blessing on your life, "You are my beloved son with whom I am well pleased."

Your High Status and Worth

The creation account clearly displays that, as God's image-bearer, you have an incredibly high status. The story of redemption shows that you are a wanted son. Like Father, like son. There is a principle of life at work here: the higher status the father and family, the higher status his children. Since there is no one higher in status than God, his offspring bear high status and worth. A man gains his worth not by what he accomplishes or how he fails. His worth is directly tied to origins.

Did your own father give you the impression you were not wanted? When you don't believe your own father wanted you, it's easy to spend your life trying to prove to yourself and others that you are worthy. But you don't have to do that anymore. Jesus's death for us proves that we are loved and wanted sons. As you learn to live out of your identity as son, instead of repeating the mistakes of the past, you will learn to live a whole new life as a son of your perfect heavenly Father. When the Father gave us life in Christ, he restored our worth and status. Knowing who you are in Christ will change your life.

The Irreplaceable Father

"I find my father everywhere . . ." The quote at the beginning of this chapter needs reinterpretation in light of the cross. While we must know our earthly father story and how it has affected us, as Christ-following men we are on a new adventure now: seeing our heavenly Father everywhere. Since the day we became Christians, the Father has been seeking to show us that our great or average or failed dads no longer ultimately define us.

Difficulties in your relationship with your earthly father are significant and have an impact. But in Christ, you have all that you need. You are accepted and loved by the one irreplaceable Father—your heavenly Father. The Sovereign Creator-Father of the universe completely defines you as his beloved son. As men made in the image of God and adopted as sons, we have been given incomparable worth and high status. We are irreplaceable to our heavenly Father.

He who is irreplaceable counts us worthy to him, and involves himself in our lives every day. Believe in *this* Father. Make *this* Father your focus. Allow *this* Father's words of love, grace, and acceptance to run through your mind and heart. Doing so will change everything. It will make you into the man you want to be and were designed to be—the kind of man the world needs.

Take It to Heart

1. Read again the quotes from men about their relationship with their fathers. Can you relate to any of them? How would you describe your relationship with your father?

2. What kind of man did you learn to be from your father? What kind of man do you not want to become from watching him?

3. Are you the man you desire to be? In what ways are you on track? In what ways would you like to develop (Philippians 2:12–13)?

4. How does living as God's son change how you view yourself and your life? What does it say about your successes? Your failures? Your relationships (Ephesians 5:22 –6:9)?

5. If you don't know God as your father, you can start a relationship with him right now by asking for

forgiveness in Jesus's name. What do John 3:16, Galatians 4:4–7, and 1 John 1:9–10 tell you about how to get to know your heavenly Father?

6. How can your walk with God be different starting now by viewing him as an engaged and loving Father?

2

The Father Who Knows You
and Is Known

"Because I know he is for me,
because I know he cares, because I know he loves me,
I can deal with almost anything. If God is in charge,
it helps a whole lot to know he is for us."[1]

Steve Brown

One assignment I always give my seminary students is to tell their life story by focusing on their experience with their fathers. I ask them to do this because what we know about our earthly fathers, what we piece together from the way they treat us, shapes who we are and what we become—after all, "like father, like son." Some stories are heartrending. One young man shared with me that his biological father had never called him "son." Here is the beginning of his story:

I was conceived in an adulterous affair. My mother was with her then-husband's best friend, somewhere in Texas, and that is where it all began for me. When my mother told my father that she was pregnant, he said, "I don't want anything to do with it."

How do you think it affected that young man to know that his own father called him, not son, but "it"? Don't get me wrong, I like "its" and have some pretty cool ones. One birthday some guys from my church surprised me with the gift of a 1911 model .45 caliber pistol. Whenever I look at it, I think of them, and I'm glad. It's one of my prize possessions. But it's not a person—it's an "it."

If you are an "it," your value is only as high as your current owner. When the owner changes, your value changes. "Its" are sold, traded, given, or thrown away. Things usually lose value over time. You put "its" on the curb for whoever wants them when you don't need them anymore. If no one picks them up, they go to the landfill. People have useless "its" they throw away all the time, and apparently this man thought my student was one of them.

The good news for that student—and for all of us—is that we have a heavenly Father who doesn't treat us as an "it." He calls you his son. He knows you inside and out as his well- loved son and he wants you to know him as your dearly loved father. Knowing that you are loved and valued as a son by the most powerful person in the world changes everything for men. Here's how the young man who entered life as an "it" got to know his heavenly Father:

Then came the nightmares. Not metaphorical nightmares but real, terrifying nightmares. Growing up with my stepfather had molded me into a person who wasn't scared of much of anything. When you get used to abuse and living underneath the cloud of threat, a certain hardness forms that takes no mustering of courage to exhibit fearlessness. But these nightmares went beyond childish night terrors. They drove me to my Bible. I read and read and read. The nightmares continued. Then one night my world changed.

It was in the evening, but still light out. I was falling asleep reading my Bible. I was in one of the Gospels. I don't remember the story; all I remember was drifting off to sleep, but then I snapped awake. It was pitch dark. I didn't have any drowsiness to shake off, there was no transition between sleep and waking. I was just awake, as if it were the middle of an ordinary day. Did I just hear something? My body was turned toward the wall, and my back was to the bedroom door. Then I did hear something, and there was no question what woke me up. I stiffened. For the third time I heard, "Steve." I could not turn over and look in the direction of the Voice. I did not want to, anyway. Instead I pulled the covers over my head, terrified. An eighteen-year-old who thought he was tough, pulling cheap, worn-out sheets over his head in hopes of avoiding the Voice and all the implications that echoed behind it. I never said a word. I just waited for . . . . something. I don't know if I was expecting to die, but I just lay there.

A wind passed over my ear through the street. It rippled the sheet and sounded, over my ear, like someone gently blowing into a microphone. Immediately all fear was gone. Not just was all fear gone, but a peace that passes understanding entered and remained. The nightmares left—never to return. My life was changed literally overnight.[2]

What had my friend heard? He heard the voice of his heavenly Father, the One who Jesus taught us to call Abba—literally "Daddy" (Mark 14:36; Galatians 4:6). Over time he learned about the love of his heavenly Father who sent his Son to die for his sins and give him a new life and a new Spirit. The voice of his heavenly Father led him to a transformed life with a wonderful wife and children of his own. You won't meet a more soft-spoken and kind man. Knowing his heavenly Father has changed everything for my friend. Instead of being chained to the past, my formerly broken friend is now a wounded healer. He has the deep peace, the shalom, that only a grace experiencer can know. The kind of peace that can only come when deep pain is met by overwhelming love, the total love of a perfect Father.

Far too many men have experienced the tragedy of being treated as an "it." After thirty years as a pastor I think I've heard it all, but then someone tells me another story that rises to my top-ten list of a father's inhumanity to his son. I also hear the stories of many men who had great dads who treated them as beloved sons. But whether you had a great father or one who treated you as an "it," no earthly father can replace a man's need for a growing relationship with his heavenly Father.

Human dads are limited and finite. They can give love, but they cannot give infinite love. They can give wisdom, but they cannot give infinite wisdom. Dads can give temporal help, but they cannot give eternal salvation. Dads can open up their lives and hearts to their sons, but they can't change their children's heart. The love of a father can help his son, but cannot transform his son. For that kind of change you must experience *the* Father.

As you grow to know your heavenly Father, you will also grow to know yourself. And that will change you from the inside out into someone who can love and open his own heart to others.

The Father Who Wants to Be Known

It's not always easy for men to be open and honest. Most of us were taught from an early age that openly expressing our feelings and sharing our struggles is not a particularly "manly" thing to do. We learn to hide who we are from an early age. This was highlighted during a study trip to the Georgia mountains when my wife Caron and I walked in the early mornings and evenings. We often saw lots of deer—all of them does. We never once saw a buck—they were all hiding. Of course, men aren't exactly like bucks. But it did remind me of guys in one way: we hide well. We can live in isolation and feel like we thrive, staying hidden and unknown. It hurts us more than we know to be this way, and it hurts our sons even more.

In heaven I hope to sit down over a cup of coffee with my earthly dad because his story was hidden from me. He wasn't able to coherently lay it out for me while he was here on earth. It was one of the reasons that I slipped and tripped at the starting line of my manhood.

I'm sure there were many reasons he was so hidden. Perhaps one factor was that he lost his dad at age eleven— an earthshaking loss for a young boy. He said more than once to me that his dad was the person most like Jesus Christ that he had ever met. When the biggest person in his life was ripped away, he must have been cut to shreds. The dangling components of his inner life never came together as he became the man of the house way too early. How would this orphan boy become a man? Would he follow in his father's footsteps as planned and become a missionary doctor too? His Venezuelan grandfather rejected him when he wouldn't stay in Venezuela and instead came to the US for medical school. World War II yanked him away to fix bodies torn by bullets and flying hot metal. The new normal of postwar Los Angeles must have been anything but normal. Marriage, two kids, a career out of medicine, divorce, remarriage, then death from cardiac arrest at eighty-seven. Unhappiness and darkness marked his life. He missed out on being a father to his son and daughter by his own decisions.

Sounds like I know a lot about him, right? Not a chance. Theories. Mostly theories. Sketchy details unwillingly given, painfully pulled out of him, told in contradictory ways over years, pieced together by the few who were near him and by his son who was trying to get his own story straight: "Who are we? Who am I again?" He was hidden and still is hidden from me. Too many men have "bucks" for dads and they just do not know their dads or themselves. Gabriel, the oldest son in the movie *The Patriot*, expressed my exasperation when he said to his father, "Strangers know more about you than I do!"

In my experience, sons want and need to know their fathers. A son that knows his father is like a sprinter with his feet firmly planted at the beginning of the race on the starting blocks. A father who lets his son know him, who opens his heart and his life to his son, acts like starting blocks for a boy. Feet firmly planted, he can move ahead more confidently and quickly in life, springing into manhood. Boys with a hidden dad slip and slide a lot at the starting point of manhood as they try to get some positive forward momentum in life.

When a son doesn't really know his father, he can't really know himself. A father who is unhidden—who shares who he is with his son without holding back anything—is able to help his son find his own point of reference and identity in a chaotic world. A father differentiates his son from the crowd, focuses him, reinforces the point that his son is unique, and points to the trails in life that are consistent with their family.

If you had an earthly father who opened his life and heart to you, you know your father's story. That's a wonderful gift. But to really know ourselves, we have to go further than our earthly fathers. We have to know *the* Father—the one who made us and knows us intimately. We have to know him. All that our own earthly fathers can do only imperfectly (or not at all), our heavenly Father does perfectly.

The good news is that our heavenly Father wants to be known. He wants his sons to know all about him because he is not hidden. He is a totally committed "all-in" Father who wants you to know him and his love for you.

Knowing Your Heavenly Father Through Creation

One way we can know God is simply by looking at what he has made. What a good way to get to know anyone. Just look at what a person creates and you will know so much about them. It's easy to take a close look at what God made—just look up. Psalm 19:1–2 says, "The heavens declare the glory of God, and the sky above proclaims his handiwork. Day to day pours out speech, and night to night reveals knowledge." God started talking from the very moment creation began and he has not stopped talking since. What do we learn about God from what he made? That question could never be fully answered, but let's just make a small start.

Whether we're hiking in the Rockies or driving to work, it's easy to see in the world around us that there is a Creator God who is unimaginably powerful (Romans 1:18–20), and who exercised endless creativity in the varieties of animals and plants he has made (Job 39). God's infinite wisdom and provision for his creatures is seen in the very foundations and boundaries of earth's sea and geography (Job 38:8–11) as well as the cycles of the days and seasons (Job 38:19–20). Mapping the human genome stuns us with the intricacy of God's design. When you look at the world around you and consider who created it, you see the power, magnificence, and glory of God, your Father.

Knowing Your Father Through the Bible

Even though we can learn much about God through what he has made, God hasn't finished revealing himself. The heavens declare the glory of God, and yet he still speaks to us through his words. He gives us the Bible because he intentionally desires to become a Father and to have a relationship with his children.

He tells us all about himself and ourselves from Genesis to Revelation. The Bible is the self-revelation of a Father who really wants to be known. He doesn't want us to misunderstand who he is. He specially selected people who would faithfully record his words, thoughts, actions, promises, and desires for his people. When I emphasize that the Bible is the one book we men need to master and let master us, some of my friends have said to me, "Pete, it's not a small book! And I don't like to read that much." I get that, but the Father talks as much as he does so as not to be hidden to his boys.

As we read the Bible, we learn that our Father's power knows no limits. He creates something out of nothing. He raises the dead to life. What he decides to do, he is able to do. That's omnipotence. You have an all-powerful Father who is all-in with his sons and daughters as well as everything else he has created. What he creates by his grace, he has the power to sustain by his grace.

We are also reminded that God knows everything about everything. That's omniscience. He knows all about you. You are unhidden to him. He knows you better than you know yourself. Knowing all there is to know about you, he's still wild about you! God tells us in the Bible that he knows when we sit, when we rise, what we are thinking at all times, and what we are going to say even before it comes out of our mouths. In fact, every day has already been planned for us by our loving heavenly Father (Psalm 139:1–4, 16).

Jesus added to that picture of heavenly care when he told his followers that even the hairs on their heard were numbered by their heavenly Father (Matthew 10:30). Your earthly father had a part in giving you life, but not every earthly father is able or even wants to faithfully care for his children. You can know for sure that God, your perfect Father, created you and will certainly not abandon you because he reminds you of that truth again and again in his words to you.

Your heavenly Father is not only all-powerful and all-knowing, he is omnipresent. God is everywhere at all times (Psalm 139). The Father is able to keep up with us all simultaneously and still give each of us his full attention. Did you ever meet someone who gave you one hundred percent of their attention? You feel like the most important person in the world when you are with them. That's the way it always is with you and God. He is listening. He will always listen.

These few paragraphs can scarcely do justice to all that the Bible teaches about our Father in heaven. It's a lifelong journey to get to know your Father, and it's the greatest adventure of all in life. My exploration into knowing God was kick-started years ago by A. W. Tozer's statement that, "What comes into our minds when we think about God is the most important thing about us."[3] Reading *Knowing God* by J. I. Packer hooked me for life in knowing God the Father.[4]

And how incredible that the Father doesn't just give us creation and words about himself, but he gives us his own Son Jesus to show us personally what his love and care look like in a broken and messed-up world. The Father who wants his children to know him sent his Son so that there would be no confusion at all about who he is and what kind of relationship he wants to have with his children.

The Father Is Known Through the Son

Here's how Jesus explains getting to know your heavenly Father:

> "If you had known me, you would have known my Father also. From now on you do know him and have seen him." Philip said to him, "Lord, show us the Father, and it is enough for us." Jesus said to him, "Have I been with you so long, and you still do not know me, Philip? Whoever has seen me has seen the Father. How can you say, 'Show us the Father'? Do you not believe that I am in the Father and the Father is in me? The words that I say to you I do not speak on my own authority, but the Father who dwells in me does his works. Believe me that I am in the Father and the Father is in me, or else believe on account of the works themselves." (John 14:7–11)

Jesus is God the Son who perfectly reveals the Father to us. Let that sink in. Grab some time and read a Gospel in one sitting. Pay particular attention to what Jesus reveals to you about the Father. To know our elder brother is to know our Father.

When we reflect on Jesus coming to this earth, we know that this unique event was motivated by love from God the Father as well as God the Son and God the Spirit. The cross reveals the love of the Father every bit as much as it declares the love of Jesus. As Jesus walked this earth, he gave a living picture of the love of the Father for his people. When we see Jesus calling his disciples by name to follow him, we see the Father's love in action (John 1:35–51).

Jesus's encounter with an enemy of his people, a Samaritan woman who obviously had a painful and tumultuous relational past gives us another picture of God's love at work (John 4). Jesus is tired and hungry, but he sees her need is more important than rest and food. So he draws her into a conversation, using language she will connect with, and answers her questions to help her connect to God. In everything Jesus does, we clearly see the love, patience, and generosity of the Father.

The Road to True Manhood

Put down the list of the five marks of manhood or whatever other list you are trying to follow in order to reach true manhood. Instead, look up at the sky and read creation to get to know your heavenly Father. Pick up your Bible and read those ancient stories with an eye to what they reveal about your God. Look to Jesus, the author and finisher of your faith. Ask the Spirit to fill you with the knowledge of God's love for you in Christ. Think much about God's love for his people and how he proved it on the cross.

Spend time thinking about how your Father wants to make himself known to his boys. How he wants his boys to have the security, peace, and joy that can only come from knowing their Father. Sit back and rest in the fact that because of Jesus you can have a deep, real, and close relationship with the all-powerful God of the universe.

Remember, because of Jesus, the Father doesn't view you as an "it." You are his beloved son, and he's all-in with you and completely for you. The more time we spend reflecting on the Father, the more time we spend getting to know him and trusting his love for us, the more we want to be and, in fact do, become like him. It's an inevitable process. Sons who are deeply loved by their fathers want to imitate their fathers out of respectful love. And they do.

"Pete, you and I are so insecure we need therapy!" my mentor Steve Brown once said to me. Because Steve not only teaches grace but he models grace, I knew he had just given me a gracious challenge to look deeper inside my soul. I am insecure. I want to prove my worth to myself and others. But knowing God as my father is changing me. Getting to know him as my father, realizing that to him I'm not an "it" but his deeply loved and known son, gives me the capacity and desire to know and love others more deeply. The Father's self-revelation and acceptance of me fuels my interest in others.

A surprising result is how much easier it is to reveal myself to others—the good, the bad, and the ugly—without wincing as much. Sometimes after I share what I am really like with someone, I inwardly smile. It's so different for me not to cover up who I really am and not to wallow in it either. I know I am a forgiven, accepted son of God. Now I am free to not guide a conversation to focus on me, but turn it to God and others. How amazing that the Father who knows me and is known is replicating himself in me. And you. Like Father, like son.

Take It to Heart

1. Does it seem to you that God is difficult to really get to know? Why?
2. What can you know about God's love for you from looking at creation (Psalm 19; Romans 1:18–20)? From reading the Bible (Psalm 119:25–32; Psalm 139)? From knowing Jesus (John 4; 14:7–11)?
3. How can knowing that you're fully known and fully loved give you the freedom to make yourself known to the key people in your life—your family, wife, children, and friends (1 Timothy 1:12–17)?
4. What are reasons it is hard to share who you really are with those around you?
5. What are some practical ways that you could make yourself known to your wife, children, friends, neighbors, and coworkers?

3

The Welcoming Father

"The supreme happiness in life is the conviction
that we are loved; loved for ourselves,
or rather, in spite of ourselves."[1]

Victor Hugo

I was hooked the moment I saw him. After the nurse cleaned him and wrapped him up into a tight cocoon, she handed him to me. There I was, face-to-face with my firstborn son, holding him like the precious gift that he is and stunned that I was blessed to be his father. Two years later I was handed another gift when another son broke the only child monopoly of his brother. Eight years later we welcomed a beautiful little girl. I felt the same with each of my children. Holding on, holding tight, embracing them for the first time, I was hooked. "This is my child," I thought fiercely, as each was handed to me on their birth day. "Nobody is going to hurt this child. No one will love them more than their mom and I will."

I was surprised by how much I wanted my children to know that I loved them. I did all of the silly things that dads do—giving smiles, hugs, and kisses, but also making unintelligible sounds and signs before they could understand language. Even without words I was communicating with them using the language of intense love, affection, and longing. Newborns need to be loved like this to thrive. Great fathers embrace their babies often and never completely stop, even after they become adults. We hug them at times when they'd rather be left alone. Sometimes our kids think we're crazy, and we are. We're crazy about them.

God our Father is never outdone by humans. His love for us is crazier and richer than the love of dads or moms. When you stop and think about it, the Father's love of his often-rebellious kids is the most amazing gift that we have. When we experience his love, we thrive. More than anything, we need his embrace. His love is better than the love you experienced or perhaps didn't experience from your own father. His love is the one thing in this world we can't do without. But how do we know we are loved by our heavenly Father? After all, we can't physically feel his embrace.

Jesus knew how much we need to know the Father's love. That's one reason he told the story of the lost son— to highlight for us the welcoming, embracing love of his heavenly Father. Read this simple story and learn about the welcoming love of your Father in heaven.

> And he said, "There was a man who had two sons. And the younger of them said to his father, 'Father, give me the share of property

that is coming to me.' And he divided his property between them. Not many days later, the younger son gathered all he had and took a journey into a far country, and there he squandered his property in reckless living. And when he had spent everything, a severe famine arose in that country, and he began to be in need. So he went and hired himself out to one of the citizens of that country, who sent him into his fields to feed pigs. And he was longing to be fed with the pods that the pigs ate, and no one gave him anything. But when he came to himself, he said, 'How many of my father's hired servants have more than enough bread, but I perish here with hunger! I will arise and go to my father, and I will say to him, "Father, I have sinned against heaven and before you. I am no longer worthy to be called your son. Treat me as one of your hired servants." ' And he arose and came to his father. But while he was still a long way off, his father saw him and felt compassion, and ran and embraced him and kissed him." (Luke 15:11–20)

Young, restless, reckless, and cocky, the younger son asks his dad for his one-third of the family estate. Since he was the second son, he knew he wouldn't get a full fifty-fifty split anyway, so why not ask for his portion now? His request meant that he didn't just want to get out of the family business; he wanted out of the family. What he was really saying to his dad was, "I wish *you* were dead, so I can get my inheritance right now." That's when inheritances are usually given right? At death? But the father overlooks his son's death wish and simply gives him what he asks for.

Not too surprisingly, the younger son spent all of his inheritance in wild living, and it just so happened that the funds ran out at the same time as an economic downturn. With no money for booze or women, or even food for that matter, this circumcised Jewish boy got a job working for uncircumcised pagans in the pig industry. In the Hebrew culture of Jesus's day where both pigs and anyone outside of the Jewish community was considered unclean, this was about as low as anyone could go.

Sometimes clarity comes to us when our foolishness has run its full course. When his hunger pangs were racking him, our young friend's situational awareness became crystal clear. Sanity arrived. He knew quite literally that his physical survival depended on his dad, the very person from whom he was asserting his freedom. Sometimes it takes starvation to give us humility, and so it was with him. He decided to go home, confess his sins, and ask to be his father's servant.

The fate of the younger son isn't the surprising part of this story—the part where we go our own way and run out of resources is all too familiar. No, the surprise ending is the welcome of the father. You might imagine that the father would reject his son—after all, the son had rejected the father. But instead, compassion floods the father's heart. In an almost unthinkable act of patriarchal self-humiliation, *the father runs to the son.* Runs, not walks. Can you picture it? Not caring who is watching, he sprints to his boy, his long lost boy who he's never stopped thinking about, the boy he has never stopped loving. The text literally says his dad "fell on his neck" and kissed him "again and again." Now that's an embrace. A son who was hopelessly lost has been found alive! "And they began to celebrate" (Luke 15:24).

What does it take to be welcomed like that by your heavenly Father? In the last chapter we discussed how God wants you to know him and how he knows you better than you know yourself. Perhaps that's not a comfort to you. You might wish that your heavenly Father did not know certain things about you. When you think of God, perhaps instead of a welcoming Father he seems like a dark, threatening cloud of judgment. In one sense you are right: there is a price to be paid for leaving the Father, striking out on our own, and going our own way instead of his way.

That's why it's so important to know that the immediate context in which Jesus is telling this story is on his way to the cross to satisfy the justice of a holy God. On the cross, Jesus paid the price for your welcome. Jesus was the perfect son who always loved the Father, the one who always did the Father's will. The Father's justice didn't have to fall on him for his own sins. Instead, he took our place. My place. Your place.

Here's the good news for prodigals who are stumbling home: all it takes to be welcomed by the Father is a simple confession of sin and trusting in Jesus's death for your righteousness. Then, just like the younger son, you are embraced, kissed, and made much of. The Father embraces you when you first come home and he never stops. The lost is found. His child has come home.

Jesus's story isn't quite over. The older brother, who represents the Pharisees of Jesus's day, is angry because the disobedient son gets a party when he returns. He thinks of himself as the good son and can't understand why the rule-breaking son is welcomed (Luke 15:28–32). The older brother simply doesn't grasp the love of the Father. He believes he can earn his father's love. That he deserves to be treated well. But God says no, "all have sinned and fall short of the glory of God" (Romans 3:23). Both older brothers (who are far from God in their pride, judgment of others, and self-righteousness) and younger brothers (who are far from God in their bad choices, addictions, and lusts) have to come home. All of us need a substitute, a Savior to graciously forgive and rescue us for our love of self, our lack of humility, and the many ways we have failed to love God and people.

When we come limping home, tired of our own way and knowing we deserve nothing, the Father is glad to give us all the rights of sons that Jesus won for us by his life, death, and resurrection. When you come home dirty, tired of sensual indulgence or self-righteous attempts to be better, and repentant, then you too are welcomed by the Father's embrace.

His embrace is more than a hug. Hugs are brief, but an embrace says, "Ah, you're home! And I'm never letting go." Because of Jesus, our sins are not counted against us. No matter what you have done or how many times you have done it, the Father welcomes you home. All it takes is a simple confession and trust in the work of another—Jesus's work for you on the cross. That's the gospel truth.

What Makes Men Tough

I've been trying to strengthen my knees with some long bike rides and to get through them I listen to music. A buddy gave me a Johnny Cash album so if you see me riding up the road with a grin on my face, it's because Johnny is singing away in my ear. Remember the song "A Boy Named Sue"? It never ceases to make me smile and pedal faster. As this ballad unfolds, the son and his dad (who named him Sue) get into an epic barroom brawl. The song ends with the father explaining to his son that he did him a favor to name him Sue because that's the reason he has "gravel in his guts and spit in his eye."

Johnny Cash is right that this world is fallen and rough and filled with pain that we cause or others cause for us. How do we get through? His song says that we get through if we get tough. I agree that boys have to learn to survive and thrive in a broken world with a lot of jagged edges that cut and slash. But what a boy needs from his father is not shame-training, but his embrace.

Even hip-hop artists who celebrate hyper-masculinity lament their absent fathers. Eminem rages against his father, "cause he split, I wonder if he even kissed me goodbye." Jay-Z sings of being "a kid torn apart once his pop disappeared." He asks the void, "Do you even remember the tender boy you turned into a cold young man?"[2]

When I talk with men, I hear those same kinds of themes. Men are struggling with work, marriage, children, and the gut-wrenching challenges of life in the twenty-first century. They are trying to learn how to be a man, yet many were abandoned by their dads and don't have a clue what it means to be a man or how to be one in all of their key roles. They are trying to figure it out on their own. Many men are crying out for the embrace of a father. Men without fathers can get really mean, but they don't get strong. But for all who come to their heavenly Father through Jesus, a warm welcome and a strengthening, lasting embrace awaits.

The Welcoming Father

Often in parenting boys, fathers focus more on getting the actions of manhood into their sons and neglect developing a relationship of love. I just read the booklet *From Boy to Man: The Marks of Manhood,* by Al Mohler.[3] Eleven marks of manhood are given and dads are reminded to see how crucial their role is in developing boys into men. Of course this is true. But our sons first need the welcoming love of their father that will give them the foundation for emotional and spiritual strength. You can't grow into a man who loves well without being well loved.

Thankfully, no matter what your relationship with your earthly father is like, because of Jesus you have access to the strongest foundation of all—the welcoming, embracing love of your heavenly Father. To be embraced by the Father, you only need to depend on Jesus and ask for forgiveness for going your own way. Those who come to God trusting in Jesus are always loved, always forgiven, and *always* welcomed. Because of Christ, nothing can separate you from the love of the Father—not your sins, not the sins of others, not trouble, not hardship, not anything in the whole world (Romans 8:37–39).

True strength comes from knowing and experiencing the unconditional love of your perfect Father. His embrace sends waves of power into his sons. Taking a cue from my tough dad, a WWII vet, I wanted to be tough too. I highly valued emotional toughness and physical strength, taking on endurance challenges to build and prove strength. My experience with walking with the Father, however, is that the greatest strength comes from his love for me. The Father's embrace keeps us from slipping into a black hole of nothingness and inferiority: of being defined by a woman's embrace so that serial monogamy or bed hopping or porn watching becomes my life in the place of a real life; or by financial success that keeps me working nonstop to get just a little bit more; or by physical strength that has to be constantly maintained in the gym and must rise to every challenge. When the Father embraces us with love, then we can love our wives, our kids, our friends, our coworkers, and others who are hurting (1 John 4:9, 16). Godly strength comes from God's embrace and enables us to be sacrificial givers rather than takers (Ephesians 5:25).

The Father's embrace keeps us from working frenetically in an attempt to feel like we are worth something. We already know we are worth everything to the Father. He gave his own Son so that we could be his sons. When we are embraced by the Father, we feel like we belong— not to this world but to the eternal God. Because of his embrace, death is no longer our enemy and heaven is our welcome destination.

Because we are loved, we aren't afraid of judgment when our bodies die. Instead of being afraid to meet a holy God in heaven, we have a new picture of what our reunion will be like. It will look a lot like when the father ran down the road to meet his prodigal son. Our heavenly Father will run to us, and we will run to him and be embraced. I suspect that right after he wipes the tears away we can expect a bear hug. Then the party will begin and never end.

Take It to Heart

1. Was your home a place where physical and verbal affection was warmly communicated? Were you embraced and accepted by your dad?

2. Read again the story of the prodigal son (Luke 15:11–32). Now rewrite the story using yourself as the younger son. Substitute your prodigal (wasteful/sinful) past into the story. Then rewrite the father's welcome with your name.

3. Have you ever found yourself acting more like the older son? What did that look like in your life? Read Philippians 3:4–6 for a picture of Paul, as the older son, before he met Jesus. What does the older son have to understand before he can experience the father's love?

4. If you really knew and experienced your heavenly Father's love, how do you think it would change the way you treat others? How you view your work? Your failures? Your successes (Romans 8:37–39; 1 John 4:9, 16)?

5. How does being confident in the Father's love help us develop honest and open friendships with other guys that could be considered "iron sharpening iron"—relationships that are authentic, motivating, and encouraging?

4

The Approval-Giving Father

"You may be insecure, inadequate, mistaken,
or potbellied. Death, panic, depression,
and disillusionment may be near you. But you are
not just that. You are accepted. Never confuse your
perception of yourself with the mystery that
you really are accepted."[1]

Brennan Manning

Tepilit, the young Masai boy, heard the lioness growl one dark night and knew that his family and their cattle were at risk. Grabbing a weapon he courageously confronted the lion and killed the huge beast. "Two months after I killed the lioness, my father summoned all of us together. In the presence of all his children he said: 'We are going to initiate Tepilit into manhood. He has proven before all of us that he can now save children and cattle.'"[2]

Masai culture has a clear path to manhood for a boy to take, but it's not an easy path. As David Gilmore explains in *Manhood in the Making: Cultural Concepts of Masculinity,* to become a man, the Masai boy must first endure circumcision without uttering a cry of pain or even blinking. He must then prove himself as a warrior and develop economic independence by accumulating property.

Gilmore wraps up his discussion of how the Masai boys become men by saying, "Their construction of manhood encompasses not only physical strength or bravery but also a moral beauty construed as selfless devotion to national identity. It embodies the central understanding that the man is only the sum of what he has *achieved* and that what he has *achieved* is nothing more or less than what he leaves behind"[3] (emphasis mine).

Although the Masai boy's path to manhood is quite different than what boys in Western culture experience, it's interesting to note what is the same—the emphasis on achievement. As Thomas Gregor says, "There are continuities of masculinity that transcend cultural differences"[4] and this means that many cultures see the roles of men in similar ways even if there are different paths to become an approved man. In most cultures, as Michael Herzfeld says in *The Poetics of Manhood*, "There is less focus on 'being a good man' and more emphasis on 'being good at being a man'—a stance that stresses performative excellence, the ability to foreground manhood by means of deeds that strikingly 'speak for themselves.'"[5]

This emphasis on manhood being measured by achievement leads many men to make their performance (and others approval of their performance) the most important thing in their lives. Perhaps you can relate to what Abraham Lincoln said while running for the Illinois State Legislature: "Every man is said to have his peculiar ambition. I have no other so great as that of being truly esteemed of my fellow men, by rendering myself worthy of their esteem. How far I shall succeed in gratifying this ambition is yet to be developed."[6]

Or what General Custer, the hero of Civil War battles and western Indian wars, wrote before he led his troops into ambush at Little Big Horn: "In years long-numbered with the past, when I was verging upon manhood, my every thought was ambitious—not to be wealthy, not to be learned, but to be great. I desired to link my name with acts and men, and in such a manner as to be a mark of honor—not only to the present, but to future generations."[7]

When Achievement and Approval Become an Addiction

When I read Lincoln's and Custer's comments on their twin goals to do something great and to have others notice, I was shocked into my own confession: I'm an addict. I am addicted to getting other's approval through my hard work. It had been going on for years, but I didn't really understand how my addiction was driving me. I had a nebulous sense that something was wrong in my life—that I was too dependent on work and others' approval—but it didn't seem like a negative thing. After all, I was doing pretty well at my job. Others thought of me as a success. But when I read Lincoln's and Custer's words for the first time I thought, *They have articulated my life's ambition. I couldn't have spoken my own thoughts that clearly. I'm addicted to my own ambitions and others' approval.*

And, like all addicts, my addiction was running my life and ruining it at the same time. For twenty-six years I served the same church as church planter and senior pastor. They were my people and I loved them. Most of my adult life I've been a senior pastor and before that was a youth pastor. I wasn't in the pastorate just for me. I was in it for Jesus and for people, but lying just below the surface was an insatiable thirst to get my worth from performance.

Even today this is a hard story for me to tell. I'm astounded that I was so clueless for so long about my addiction and how it hurt others. No doubt my drive to achieve and be noticed by others for my achievements hurt my wife the most. The decision to enter the pastorate was more by my prodding than a mutually well-prayed-through decision. I grimace as I write this, but I practically bullied her into the pastorate.

And, as a pastor, I often put my need to be approved by church members above the needs of my family (notice I didn't say their *actual* needs, but *my* need for their approval). I remember one day when our first son was young and Caron asked me if I could come home and watch him while she ran an errand. My response was that I had too much work to do to come home. Later I confessed to her that the truth was that I feared someone from our church would stop by the office, find it locked, and then criticize me as one of those pastors who was doing the bare minimum because "pastors really only work one day a week." I sent a message to her loud and clear: my work is more important than you.

My pressure to perform put my wife on notice to perform and made her feel unworthy, unloved, and conditionally accepted. If it were not for my courageous wife, I would have put performance expectations on my kids too, but they were largely spared from a work- addicted dad.

In the long run, worth from approval kept me from investing in closer relationships with other men and fostered a loner mentality. Since the work of the church is never done, being busy brought admiration and helped build an active church, but inhibited my capacity to make hard decisions, build deeper relationships with staff and leaders, and no doubt sent messages of disapproval to staff who didn't work as hard as I did or whose "results" were not up to my standards.

Nothing I did in ministry could satisfy my constant, never-ending desire for others' approval. You can't keep that up forever and eventually fuel for my work was gone. I couldn't keep going as a pastor. I was burned out. I had to let go of my work because in the end it wasn't about serving Jesus as much as it was about trying to build my own kingdom where I would be noticed, approved, and accepted. My desires to focus on reaching men help me let go of a role that after years only fed me guilt, shame, and emptiness. That's difficult to write, but it was a grace to run out of gas and to hear the Father say, "Son, it's time. I'm lifting the weight." He lifted the burden and has been calling me to freedom from work-induced worth ever since.

Perhaps you can relate? You too have learned to measure your manhood by what you achieve and by what others think about your achievements. But what a precarious foundation on which to build your worth. Timothy Keller calls this, "The crushing burden of working primarily to prove" our worth.[8] What lengths we go to in order to gain the esteem of others and to prove our worth as men!

How We Get Hooked on Performance

We get some of the fuel toward performance naturally. God created Adam in his image, to be his son. That was his core identity. Brought into existence by a God who desired a relationship with him, Adam found great worth. Secondarily, God called Adam to be a leader-worker-provider (Genesis 1:26; 2:15). We were created to be sons of God who would live out our roles as sons in leading, working, and providing.

But because sin entered the world, we become disconnected from our identity as sons, and our calling to be workers also becomes broken and twisted. No longer able to find our acceptance and approval in our relationship with our heavenly Father, we turn to work as the primary way to find acceptance and approval. If we don't have a relationship with our heavenly Father, it makes sense to try to fill up the father sinkhole with work. Without our core identity as sons of God, our significance is tied to our successes, and success comes primarily through achievement.

Dads who themselves are struggling to achieve and wanting approval often set the bar high for their sons as well. We learn quickly that when we perform as desired, we get words of affirmation, "Good job. You did well." Or maybe it's only a subtle nod, a slight smile. But to sons looking for a father's approval, that's enough to get the point across—when you perform as expected, you earn your father's approval.

Then of course there are so many men who grew up, like I did, without their father. Almost two decades ago I read David Blankenhorn's landmark book, *Fatherless America: Confronting Our Most Urgent Social Problem*. He argued that "Fatherlessness is the most harmful demographic trend of this generation. . . . If this trend continues, fatherlessness is likely to change the shape of society."[9]

Sadly, Blankenhorn's insights have become the reality for many. Fatherlessness increased in America during WWII with so many dads gone to war, dying in war, or returning from war hardly able to function as dads. And that trend has only increased in the last decades. Many men today are without a father to affirm them, love them, approve of them, guide them into manhood, and pronounce that they are men. Without a dad guys are even more vulnerable to trying to find their worth in an endless cycle of approval-performance.

There are so many ways that boys learn this lesson. When I realized achievement could be translated into significance, I became a Cub Scout. Do the work and earn a badge! They'll present it to you at a special ceremony, and then you can wear the badge on a shirt so that you and everyone can see your accomplishments. That snowballed into badges earned as a Boy Scout and on into adulthood. I collected and displayed so many symbols of achievement that it became embarrassing. I needed these achievements to satisfy the little boy's emptiness. They didn't, of course. Achievements are like drugs: they last for a short time, demand more and bigger doses, but always leave you empty.

Getting Certifiably Approved

What breaks into this cycle of performance-approval? What can deliver us from the uncertainty and the never-ending work of trying to find our significance in what we do? We need to go back to our heavenly Father. He is our perfect Father whose approval makes all the difference in the world. We need him to put his hand on our shoulders and say, "Alright son, slow down. You're hustling like your worth depends on your work and it's killing you! Relax. Rest in the peace that comes from knowing that I approve of you because of Jesus. That's final. Accept my assessment of you and stop trying to get it from people.

Their approval doesn't matter. My approval defines you forever."

How do you know that your heavenly Father is really saying that to you? Because he tells you so in the Bible.

> But now the righteousness of God has been manifested apart from the law, although the Law and the Prophets bear witness to it—the righteousness of God through faith in Jesus Christ for all who believe. For there is no distinction: for all have sinned and fall short of the glory of God, and are justified by his grace as a gift, through the redemption that is in Christ Jesus, whom God put forward as a propitiation by his blood, to be received by faith. (Romans 3:21–25)
>
> Therefore, since we have been justified by faith, we have peace with God through our Lord Jesus Christ. (Romans 5:1)
>
> There is therefore now no condemnation for those who are in Christ Jesus. (Romans 8:1)

When you understand what these verses are saying, then you will know the approval you want and desperately need from your heavenly Father. The official seal from the Father that you are satisfactory, acceptable, and approved is yours because of what Jesus has done for you. The hard work to gain your Father's approval has already been accomplished. There is nothing left for you to do.

In Romans 3, Paul gives us the bad news and the good news. The bad news is that what we have feared our entire lives is true—that we fall short. We haven't done enough. We can't do enough. No matter how hard we try. No matter what we accomplish, we will never measure up to God's standards for us. We have been examined and found to be sinners. Our never-ending struggle for approval, significance, and success all stems from this one central truth: we fall short. That's why no success, no work, no affirmation from any human satisfies. We are doomed to always work and never to rest.

But there is good news. Someone has done for us what we could not do. Jesus lived the perfectly right life that we could not. We are flawed. He is righteous. He always loved God and people perfectly, not just in what he did, but what he thought and felt. When we put our faith in him, his perfect life becomes ours—"the righteous of God through faith in Jesus Christ for all who believe" (Romans 3:22).

The approval we desire is available to us by faith in Jesus. Because he paid the price for our sins, we are justified. That means God has declared us, "Not guilty." We are loved and graciously gifted with the full righteousness of Christ through God-given faith. We are officially pronounced not guilty by the Father of any and all sin, and we are acquitted of all charges against us for all time and eternity. To be *justified* brings peace with God—a sense of "shalom" or well-being that fills our lives. Because of the cross, all is well with you and God. What a relief from "the crushing burden" of always trying to prove our worth.

Guilt and Grace

Whether acknowledged or not, we know deep in our hearts that we don't measure up. We feel the lack of our Father's approval and so we set out to get it ourselves—we work, we strive for acceptance and significance, but we are never satisfied. No human approval can ever substitute for approval from our heavenly Father. The result is that a black cloud of guilt hangs over our lives. Guilt is often the unrecognized motivator in what we say and do—it leads us to try harder and work harder to measure up (what the Bible calls works righteousness).

But the solution is not trying harder—it's resting on what Christ has done for us. That's why we must allow the truth of the gospel that Jesus paid it all and did it all to soak through to our masculine work ethic. We need to remember every day that nothing we do, achieve, accomplish, or make can erase our guilt and provide worth. Only the righteousness of Christ can undo, wipe way, and remove guilt before our holy Father—Jesus's sacrifice on the cross has accomplished it!

"It is finished," Jesus said. On the cross his work for us was finished, and through faith in him, our guilt is finished, removed "as far as the east is from the west" (Psalm 103:11–12). Because of the cross, "There is now therefore no condemnation for those who are in Christ Jesus" (Romans 8:1).

When you come to Jesus for forgiveness, instead of living with guilt as a black cloud over your life, it becomes a reminder that you are a sinner who needs to daily ask for forgiveness and daily claim Christ's perfect record (his righteousness) as your own. As a Christian, you have the Spirit of Christ, so you will be convicted and reminded when you are doing something wrong. That's a good thing!

God-given guilt has four elements:

1. A clear violation of the law
2. Recognition of guilt for that violation
3. Punishment
4. Release or freedom from the guilt of the violation

Perhaps an example from my early days as a really bad teenage driver will help to explain how guilt works. A few days after I got my license, I was speeding down the streets in Long Beach, California, going fifty in a thirty-five-mile-an-hour zone. A policeman's radar gun proved I was in violation. I felt the guilt of that violation as I was pulled over. I was punished for that violation when the judge suspended my license for ten days. When those ten days were over, the punishment was lifted and I had wheels again. I was free to drive.

The same dynamic is true in our lives. When we get honest with ourselves, we know we have violated God's law of love, and we fear the punishment we deserve. But the gospel frees us from our punishment. When you become a Christian, you recognize that you are a sinner, but you don't pay for your sins. Jesus took your punishment, so without you doing anything, the guilt is gone, grace is given, and worth is restored. When you have a black cloud of unresolved guilt, you never experience release from the guilt.

Because of God's grace to you in sending his Son to die for your sins, you can breathe easy. Knowing you are forgiven in Christ means you can daily and quickly acknowledge to God that you are a sinner who needs forgiveness. You can bring your workaholism to God and request forgiveness. And daily you will receive forgiveness and love from your heavenly Father. Not based on your efforts, but based on what Jesus has done for you. This is God's grace. Grace is receiving what you don't deserve when there is every evidence that you deserve the opposite. Look up and see the face of an approving and beaming Father. Ambition of our own never fills our souls. Approval from the Father always will.

The world does, of course, need men who are not only good men, but good at being men. We need quality, skilled, and diligent workers, creators, artists, and professionals, who make our world a better and more beautiful place by what they contribute. We like to work just like our Father likes to work! And we have been called to work (Genesis 1:28). We love the fulfillment that comes from a job well done, beauty created, people helped, and good accomplished. God does call us to work to care for ourselves and help others (2 Thessalonians 3:10; Ephesians 4:28).

Now, as a man with your relationship with your heavenly Father restored, you can step into your role as worker in God's world with freedom and joy. You are not trying to prove anything to family, friends, coworkers, neighbors, or anyone else! Your approval is secure in what Jesus did for you at the cross. Your Father's benediction on Jesus, "This is my beloved Son in whom I am well pleased," is also the benediction on your life. You can try and fail because your approval is secure. You can work for something bigger and richer than status or money. You can pile up riches in heaven. You can be rich toward God and others. Your life is not bound by getting ahead and proving that you are better than anyone. You are a forgiven and free man. Now you can do your work as unto the Lord because it is the Lord Christ you are serving (Colossians 3:24).

Take It to Heart

1. What do you turn to for comfort or approval when you're feeling afraid of failure, empty, and/ or defeated? Who does Psalm 46 teach us to turn toward when we are afraid?

2. In what ways are you running out of gas?

3. Describe the difference the Father has made in your life by giving you the righteousness of Christ (Romans 3:21–25). Write down three ways your

life would change if you remembered every day that in Christ you are already approved and found worthy. For example, how would your approach to work change? How would you relate to your co-workers? How would what you talk about change?

4. List the goals you have been working toward. How many of those goals are motivated by trying to prove yourself and your worth? What new goals can you brainstorm that would be about loving God and people (Psalm 103:1–14)?

5. Do you know some guys you can talk to without having to compete with them? List a few names and then consider contacting them.

5

The Identity-Building Father

"We have the choice of two identities:
the external mask which seems to be real . . .
and the hidden, inner person who seems to us
to be nothing, but who can give himself eternally
to the truth in whom he subsists."[1]

Thomas Merton

Do not mess with Angel Garcia's son Danny. Danny Garcia became the undefeated US junior welterweight boxing champion and he would say that his dad is the reason. When he was young, Danny spent his time throwing punches and ducking clear of jabs and hooks thrown at him by imaginary opponents. Angel saw the fighter in Danny, and when the boy was seven, training began at the Harrowgate Boxing Club in North Philly. Soon Danny was 25-0 as a pro.

But like I said, don't mess with Angel by messing with Danny. *Sports Illustrated* gives the inside scoop: "Want to get Angel Garcia angry? Criticize Danny Garcia. Tell him Danny can't win. That's what Kendal Holt did. At a press conference Holt sneered at a roomful of reporters and said that Danny's promoter, Golden Boy, had made a mistake making the fight. Angel seethed. At the next press event, Angel blew up cursing at Holt and screaming at him on the dais. Danny loved it. 'He's just being himself,' says Danny. 'He yells like that all the time. Why do I care if he does it at a press conference?'"[2]

Danny's got a tougher-than-nails dad, and he's become a tougher-than-nails, successful boxer because of it. The champ has a dad who believes in him one hundred percent, who doesn't talk about *if* his son will win, but *when* his son will win. The son is confident because the father built confidence into him. The son knows what he is about because the father saw the potential in him and developed that potential. Angel built a strong identity into his son. Whatever other questions Danny might have about his life, he is certain of one thing—he is a boxer that can win. We might not agree with Angel's goals for his son or his way of getting his son to fulfill those goals, and I certainly wouldn't want Angel as my father, but one thing is for sure—his son Danny doesn't have to struggle or question his identity. He knows who he is because his father has given him his identity. This father has a passion for his son!

Your Core Identity as a Son of God

Contrast that with what I heard from three young men I met in the St. Louis airport who struck up a conversation with me while we were all waiting to board.

As they started to tell me about their lives, I said to them, "Okay, you guys are in your twenties, so tell me about your generation." One of them said (while the rest nodded their heads), "In our generation guys are passive, all of us feel entitled, and we've been lied to."

"Tell me about that!" I replied. They went on to say that most guys their age struggle with knowing what it means to be a man. Also they aren't taking charge of their lives and instead are passively waiting for life and career to happen for them. Instead of pursuing a wife they're perfectly happy to have female friends as they await the perfect woman to magically appear.

They also mentioned that, along with passivity, an attitude of entitlement was epidemic among their peers. Their peers feel that they deserve to be given good jobs and incomes, but that hasn't happened. "Our professors lied to us. They told us we'd get great jobs after college but there aren't any!" Eventually they shared that they were Christians who had started a business to help other young men combat passivity, entitlement, and a harsh economic reality.

Where do young men, like my airport friends, learn how to be men? Many Christians are simply saying that men need to "step up and be men." Author Elisabeth Elliot tells men, "First off, be a man. I've said that in a hundred ways, but I'll say it again. You expect her to be a real woman, but you can't expect that if you're not a real man."[3] Others calling for manliness offer challenges from past generations like this famous one from Amos

Bronson Alcott: "First find the man in yourself if you will inspire manliness in others."

This all sounds great, but even if you were willing "to be a man" and/or "find the man in yourself," how would you know what that means? Biblically speaking, it's not "step up and be a man"; it's find your identity first as sons of the living God and become like his son and your brother Jesus. Then, by the power of his Spirit, live out your particular calling as a man. It's what God the Father is all about: making men of his boys. Call it the grace of turning boys into men.

Because of God's irresistible call to become his sons our *core identity* is about who we are in Christ. Our core identity as sons will never change in all our transitioning roles and callings as men. That's what Paul so powerfully teaches in his rapid fire, Trinitarian praise to God for our salvation in Ephesians 1. Because of the cross, the Father has blessed us with "every spiritual blessing" (1:3). God's love motivated him to adopt us as sons "through Jesus Christ" (1:5) and so we are "in the Beloved" (1:6), his family, with the same status as Jesus, the firstborn son.

Paul says that because of Jesus's sacrifice, we have been purchased by God and forgiven of all our sins (1:7–8). Grace has been "lavished" on us so that we've heard the truth and been enabled to believe. Before we only inherited death, but now, because of our faith in Christ, we inherit life (1:8–12). Is this hard for you to believe? Paul goes on to say that we know it's true because we have been given the Spirit "who is the guarantee of our inheritance" until we see the Father face-to-face (1:13–14).

In Christ we have all the identity we need right now. Our identity is as firstborn sons of the living God. In Christ, we are the beloved sons of God in whom he is well pleased. I've been told that in Europe the first question you'll be asked after your name is "Where are you from?" In America you'll be asked "What do you do?" For us as Christians however the big identity marker is "Who is your Father?" When Captain Jerry Coffee, a pilot shot down during the Vietnamese war, stepped into his prison cell, he said to himself, "I'm going to get to know the two persons I don't know very well: God and myself."[4] That's exactly what we need. When the Father bestows the highest possible status on us by indelibly marking us as *his* firstborn sons with all the blessings that entails, then we know ourselves.

Identity in Action

Our identity as sons of God isn't just theoretical; it's meant to be lived out in the real world where we reside, work, and form relationships. We need to know how to live out our identity as sons of God in every aspect of life. Our heavenly Father has given us the Bible to teach sons of God how to live—what they do and how they do it.

God's Sons Are Called to Be Leaders

The Bible teaches us that men are called to lead in the family and in the church. I know that the idea of male leadership is controversial today, but I believe it is rooted in God's command to Adam and Eve to have dominion (rule) over the earth (Genesis 1:26). Although they were called to be partners in this, Adam was created first and the Lord gave Adam the peculiar role of being finally responsible for decisions made by both he and Eve. Some theologians call this the *Federal Headship* of Adam or just "headship."[5]

Adam's lead role in the family is highlighted by what God says to him after he eats the forbidden fruit: "And to Adam he said, 'Because you have listened to the voice of your wife and have eaten of the tree of which I commanded you, "You shall not eat of it," cursed is the ground because of you; in pain you shall eat of it all the days of your life'" (Genesis 3:17). It's clear that God held Adam, as the leader in his family, responsible for the action that introduced sin into the world. Paul, in the New Testament, also affirms Adam's ultimate responsibility in Romans 5:12, 14, and 1 Corinthians 15:22. Paul calls men as husbands and fathers to lead their families, just as Christ loved the church and gave himself up for her (Ephesians 5:22–26; 6:1–4).

Of course, affirming male leadership does not mean that women cannot or do not lead. Nor does it mean that men are never under the authority of women. Also, I am not saying women have no responsibility for their actions. Eve was culpable for her sin too. But I am saying that God calls men, whom he has gifted with greater physical strength than women, to lead their families (and in other roles in the church and at their workplace where they are called to leadership) by using their strength to protect and care for those who are weaker. If you are called to be a leader, then God wants you to lead as a sacrificial influencer for the glory of God and for the good of others.

After the fall and all through ancient times until now, there has been a sad history of men using their superior strength to oppress and take advantage of others, rather than lead responsibly. After sin corrupted the world, leaders used their status to subjugate others instead of to serve.

How do Christian men avoid the trap of using leadership as a way to get what they want and take what they want? You look to Jesus—the perfect man and perfect example of leadership. When Jesus entered space and time, he restored leadership. Instead of lording it over others, Jesus taught his disciples that a leader must be the chief servant. One day, as his disciples walked home, they were bickering about who would be first in the new kingdom that Jesus was bringing to earth. Jesus used their jockeying for position as a powerful teaching moment, "What were you discussing on the way?" he asked. You could have heard a pin drop in the room. No one wanted to respond to Jesus because they were arguing about which one of them was the greatest (Mark 9:33–37).

As Tony Campolo put it, "Most people play power games," and the disciples were certainly playing games here.[6] We use and misuse power to control people, often in order to gain status by proving that we are superior to them; that we are the greatest. Taking charge of the situation, Jesus said to his disciples who were confused about their identity and the proper use of power, "If anyone would be first, he must be last of all and servant of all" (Mark 9:35). Using a little child, who was typically undervalued in that culture, as an example of someone the disciples ought to serve and receive, Jesus taught them (and us) God's original intent for leadership.

Jesus wanted all of his disciples (present and future) *not* to use their status as sons of God to manipulate or prove their worth, but to live out their identity by serving the lowly, the weak—those who can't help themselves or repay. This is the way of true greatness and proper leadership for us when we are called to lead. The gospel changes everything, including our role as leaders.

Going on to teach the disciples more about servant-leadership, Jesus utters these unforgettable words: "You know that the rulers of the Gentiles lord it over them, and their great ones exercise authority over them. It shall not be so among you. But whoever would be great among you must be your servant, and whoever would be first among you must be your slave, even as the Son of Man came not to be served but to serve, and to give his life as a ransom for many"(Matthew 20:25–28). Jesus restored leadership to God's original design, and in so doing he condemned passivity and entitlement. Passivity might be defined "I don't know what to do so I won't do anything." Entitlement could be described "I deserve others to do for me and give me what I want." Either way is opposed to the kind of leadership Jesus modeled and the New Testament teaches (Philippians 2:1–11). God's sons follow his Son in sacrificial leadership.

God's Sons Are Called to Be Workers and Providers

As leaders and influencers of our families, churches, and culture, the Father's sons are also workers and providers. This is a *creation ordinance*, a reality established by the Father from the beginning. "The LORD God took the man and put him in the Garden of Eden to *work* it and keep it" (Genesis 2:15, emphasis mine). Adam was called by God to work *before* sin entered the scene. That men and women were made to work together ought to give us joy. There seems to be, however, a unique aspect for men and work in the world.

"Although God delegated authority over the earth to both the man and the woman," writes Larry Crabb, "it is difficult to escape the impression that God intended the man to move into the world in a way that differed from his intention for the woman."[7] Notice that after the fall, the curse on the man centered on him as he "worked in the world,"[8] the judgment on the woman focused more on "her relationship with the man."[9] As we look at the woman of excellence in Proverbs 31 we see what a diligent, intelligent, and effective worker she is, yet we also see that she is particularly oriented toward the success of her home and family. Of course, many women find their contributions in the marketplace extremely rewarding, as do men.

It seems from Scripture that men are to find one of their main callings as work in the world, and we feel particular delight and fulfillment in working "out there" in tending, creating, and building the culture for God's glory and people's good. As we reject passivity and the childish desire to be taken care of by others and produce vital results in the world for our family, we grow as men and feel an enormous joy as workers. God delights in working and is always working (John 5:17). Like Father, like son. Work is more difficult after the fall to be sure, but it is still good.

There is so much more to say about work, but my point here is that the Father helps his sons understand what it means to be a man by showing us that as leaders who reject passivity at home, we also move actively into the world to find areas where we can work and thus provide for the basic needs of ourselves, our families, and others. This is incredibly rewarding to a man.

God's Sons Are Called to Be Warriors

Calling men to be warriors may seem strange in our time and culture, yet it has biblical authority. "The LORD God took the man and put him in the garden of Eden to work it and *keep* it" (Genesis 2:15, emphasis mine). The word *shamar* (keep) in the original Hebrew carries the idea of to "guard and protect," so that Richard Phillips can legitimately write, "We're [men] not only to wield the plow but to bear the sword. . . . To be a man is to stand up and be counted when there is danger or other evil."[10]

Old Testament expert Bruce Waltke, referring to the word *shamar,* says this "term entails guarding the garden against Satan's encroachment (Genesis 3:1–5). As priest and guardians of the garden, Adam and Eve should have driven out the serpent, instead it drives them out."[11] Apparently from the very moment of their creation, Adam and Eve had the important role of guarding what God had made from his only enemy, Satan.

After the fall, evil spread. God's enemies multiplied, and his sons and daughters, to be true to him, had to step up in faithful obedience and resistance against evil. Sin quickly turned men from worshipers into murderers like Cain and hyper-masculine aggressors like Lamech, who was out to take whatever he could for himself (Genesis 4). Yet, throughout biblical history, there was always a remnant of men and women, God's own people, who were called to resist evil, protect the weak, and be a part of God's redemptive plan to save the world through his Son Jesus.

A great example of this is David, the shepherd boy who eventually became king of Israel. In 1 Samuel 17 we read about the young shepherd David, who was weak in himself, but believed that his strong God would protect him. To King Saul, David says,

"Your servant used to keep sheep for his father. And when there came a lion, or a bear, and took a lamb from the flock, I went after him and struck him and delivered it out of his mouth. And if he arose against me, I caught him by his beard and struck him and killed him. Your servant has struck down both lions and bears, and this uncircumcised Philistine shall be like one of them, for he has defied the armies of the living God." And David said, "The LORD who delivered me from the paw of the lion and from the paw of the bear will deliver me from the hand of this Philistine." (vv. 34–37)

David killed a giant that day, literally. Notice he didn't do that relying on his own strength, but on the God who was keeping him. As God delivers us, we also are given his strength to deliver others. Who might God be calling you to keep?

Of course, the greatest warrior—the one who conquered sin and death, is Jesus Christ. Jesus confronted evil head-on all through his earthly ministry, and yet taught us to turn the other cheek as he did. Telling Peter to sheath the sword, Jesus surrendered to death on our behalf and accomplished our salvation in a way that does not appear masculine to us now, nor did it to his contemporaries. But Jesus really is the model warrior as he fought for his people by laying down his own life.

We are likewise called to fight for God's glory by laying down our lives. We expend ourselves for the good of our wives, our children, our church, and our world. We fight against anything that doesn't bring God glory—domestic violence, sexual abuse, our own sins and lusts. It's all part of being a warrior in God's kingdom. To miss the warfare motif in the New Testament is to miss a significant reality of how the gospel advances (Ephesians 6:10–20).

Like Father, Like Son

As sons of God, we are no longer defined by our culture or our relationship with our fathers (or lack of relationship). Instead we are defined by our heavenly Father and our relationship with him. As his sons we are given the power of the Spirit to resemble our heavenly Father. What an incredible joy it is for a man to know that his Father is a leader, provider, and warrior and that we are called to imitate him in those key roles as his sons! In ancient times, a man took his name from his father. For example, King David was called the son of Jesse. Usually a boy also took on the same role as his father. The son of a farmer was a farmer as well.

Now, as sons of God, we take our name and our roles from our Father. God is sovereign—he is *the* King of heaven and earth. He is God Almighty, the leader without equal or even near equal. Like Father, like son.

Because of Jesus, we are sons of the living God and as our Father leads, we seek to lead like him. God is the identity-bestowing Father who, through Christ, makes his boys sons and progressively into men who sacrificially lead and fight for others the way he does.

Now, some great news: When we see what our Father is like and what he has set before us to *do* as men, it's freeing and energizing! It changes us. Instead of being passive, instead of wanting others to serve us, instead of waiting for someone to help those around us, our goal becomes to lead and fight like he leads and fights. The Father gives us our identity as sons, and by grace through the power of the Spirit, we step into our calling as leaders, workers, and warriors.

A perfect Father gives his sons a perfect identity, one that matches perfectly with who we were designed to be in God's original intent. A self-constructed identity will eventually self-destruct. But an identity bestowed by our Father in heaven will last forever. We do not need to, and in fact cannot, create our own identity. Simply go to the Father through Jesus Christ and live as a dearly beloved son.

Take It to Heart

1. What identity did your father (or the significant man in your life) give you? How has that affected your choices? Your actions? Your dreams about

the future? Take some time to write down your ideas about your identity and your father's part in how that was formed.

2. How does the good news that Jesus died and rose again connect to restructuring your identity? How much time does it take for a new identity to form in us (Ephesians 2:1-10)?

3. Describe how knowing who you are as God's son affects your choices, your actions, your dreams about the future (Mark 9:33–37)?

4. In what ways has God called you to live out your identity as his son? How does your identity as a son change your view of living out your roles as a leader, worker, and warrior (Ephesians 4:17–32)?

5. List some ways that Christian men can help each other keep focused on their new identity as the Father's sons (John 13:14; Romans 12:10; Ephesians 3:20–21; Philippians 2:3; 1 Peter 5:5)?

6

The Freedom-Giving Father

"Let us learn, therefore, to magnify this our liberty, which no emperor, no prophet, no, nor any angel from heaven has obtained for us, but Jesus Christ the Son of God, by whom all things were created both in heaven and earth."[1]

Martin Luther

It's irresistible to men of all ages. When Steppenwolf's 1968 classic song "Born to Be Wild" comes on the radio, the almost universal urge is to roll down the windows, crank up the sound, and sing along. I like to sing the loudest when I get to the chorus.

The idea of being "wild" taps into our psyche, doesn't it? When I hear that song, something inside me responds, *I'm a man. I want to be wild and do all of those things that make me feel wild and alive! I wasn't born to sit around, be domesticated, take orders, and do boring work.*

But, as a Christian man, when I get down to the last verse of this song, I wonder if I *should* like those words. Why? One reason is that the Bible tells me that I'm not "nature's child." We are not just descendants of some chemical ooze that climbed out of a primordial soup billions of years ago and just happened to turn into men. We are the intentional and very special creation of the all-powerful and all-loving God. I like the idea of "born to be wild," but when I check it against the creation account in Genesis it simply does not fit. But, although "wild" doesn't describe our original condition before the fall in Genesis 3, it sure fits our condition *after* the fall.

In Genesis it becomes clear that after the fall we actually *are* born to be wild. After Adam and Eve rebelled against God, all of their children, grandchildren, great-grandchildren, right on down to us inherited from them an internal operating system that defaulted away from obeying and enjoying God. We have all inherited their knee-jerk response to run from God's authority. When we hear what God wants, we wildly head in the opposite direction.

King David, the warrior-poet who lived about 1000 AD in the rough and tumble days of early Israel, said this when confessing his wildness to God: "Behold, I was brought forth in iniquity, and in sin did my mother conceive me" (Psalm 51:5).

Psalm 51 was written by David out of the personal shattering caused by his own wild behavior that unfolded in 2 Samuel 11—12. When he writes this psalm of repentance, he still seems to be reeling from his multiple sins. How could he have done what he did? David's only explanation for his adultery, lies, conspiracy, murder, and cover-up is that he was born with a fatal flaw—sin. What other explanation could there be? David was so blind to his sins that it took the gutsy prophet Nathan to confront him and bring him to his spiritual senses. David's personal confession that he was born to sin is echoed throughout the Bible (Jeremiah 17:9; Romans 3:9–13; 5:12; Ephesians 2:1). Like all of us, David was born to be wild, but that didn't turn out to be a good thing.

We see wildness all around us, don't we? Wildness is men who go on a shooting rampage, who steal, who are abusive, who leave their wives after twenty-five years of marriage, who abandon their children . . . . the list of the bad stuff men do is endless. As a pastor for more than thirty years, I have heard so many confessions from men about their wildness that I am hardly ever shocked (but of course still saddened). And I could tell you some stories of my own wildness that might shock you.

Wildness is the result of the fall: It is sin, and sin destroys us. We can trace wildness all through the Bible. It's Cain who murdered his brother Abel. It's Jacob's sons who sold their brother Joseph into slavery in Egypt. Wildness is the priest Eli's sons, Hophni and Phineas, who stole the best sacrificial steaks for themselves and seduced the women who served God in the temple. The list goes on and on. You can also trace wildness in your life, can't you? The times you went your own way and said yes to a desire that hurt someone else. The times when you too acted out the song "Born to Be Wild" and ended up hurting yourself and others.

But here is the good news: You *are* born to be wild, but you were *originally* created to be free! Think about it. The idea that "I can do it my way" puts us into a downward spiral of manhood-destroying slavery to sin. God wanted better for his sons. He created us to be free from sin, to love and serve him and others, to work and create while we manage a perfect world. That's the way life was supposed to be. Wildness is not next to manliness; freedom is. We are born to be wild, but originally we were forged to be free. So the important question is, how can we get back our freedom?

What Will You Do Without Freedom?

"What will you do without freedom?" William Wallace (as acted by Mel Gibson in the movie *Braveheart*) yells out to the Scots, mobilizing them to battle the British. On the scaffold just before he is killed he yells, "Freedom!" That question resounds in our own lives, doesn't it? What will we do without freedom? Only live enslaved to our own desires and fail as men. The cry "Freedom!" rings in our ears, clears our mind, and starts our hearts racing. We know that to be free is to really live.

Freedom is central to the gospel. Jesus came to this earth and lived as a free man. He was the only one since Adam who wasn't "born to be wild." He freely loved his heavenly Father and all of those around him. Then he freely offered his life in place of ours. Wild men and women deserve death. Jesus paid the price and bought our freedom.

How does Jesus's life, death, resurrection, and eventual return set us free? Here's a short list (not exhaustive, of course), but just a beginning primer on the biblical freedom the gospel brings:

Gospel Freedom Is *Freedom from Condemnation*

Ever since the fall, men (and woman) have lived in fear of death and condemnation. Even when we deny it, deep in our hearts we know that we haven't measured up, that "all have sinned and fall short of the glory of God" (Romans 3:23). The physical death that entered the garden long ago, the hiding in fear from God's justly deserved condemnation, is still played out in our lives today. The fear of death keeps us all enslaved. We know we are in danger before a holy God. Christians today don't usually like to talk too much about the living death of separation from God that the Bible calls hell. Still, it casts a dark shadow over life. We feel the weight, don't we?

But Christ frees us from condemnation and fear of punishment, and frees us to be close to our heavenly Father forever. Jesus promises that all who believe in him will not perish, but have eternal life (John 3:16). Jesus's death, burial, and resurrection evaporate the fear of condemnation for the believer, "There is therefore now no condemnation for those who are in Christ Jesus. For the law of the Spirit of life has set you free in Christ Jesus from the law of sin and death" (Romans 8:1–2). The "law of sin and death" is simply this: those who sin without a Savior die forever. They are separated from their Father and all others while enduring God's just wrath for eternity. Jesus brings freedom from such a curse. And there is more.

Gospel Freedom Is *Freedom from Self-Justification*

No more trying harder to be better. As far back as I can remember, I experienced fear of my father's punishment for my misdeeds. The only time I heard appreciation and acceptance from him was when I helped him with one of his personal projects. The message I constantly received was, "If you mess up, don't get caught! *And* you'd better achieve a lot if you want to be worth anything." Trying harder to perform well and fear of failure were my constant companions. When I became a Christian, without realizing it I applied those lessons from my earthly father to my heavenly Father. For me that meant trying really hard to obey God in all the ways the Bible said I should.

It took a long time for me to understand that I could never measure up to God's standards and that my only hope was the forgiveness Jesus purchased for me on the cross. Luther said something really profound about this tendency to perform for God by trying to keep his law. He said that our reason "far prefers the righteousness of the law before the righteousness of faith" and "this pernicious opinion that the law justifies is deeply rooted in man's reason, and all mankind is so wrapped in it that it can hardly get out."[2] So true! Our sin-broken thinking constantly returns to the (wrong) logic that our works equal gained righteousness. We try to clean ourselves up in order to be acceptable to God.

But true Christianity is never "Jesus and _____" for salvation. The gospel heart of the Christian faith is that we *cannot* make ourselves right. We are wild by nature. In fact, God calls us spiritually dead (Ephesians 2:1). We need help from outside ourselves that only Jesus offers. By faith we depend completely on him.

Since the beginning of Christianity, people have been trying to go back to a religious system to make themselves right with God and each other. In the letter to the Galatians Paul writes to those who, under the influence of Jewish teachers of the law, wanted to go to a system of "Jesus *and* the Law" for their justification from sin. Paul rightly sees their faith collapsing under the weight of the laws they are trying to keep to make themselves right with God. He is upset because he knows that this is going back to slavery (Galatians 1:6–7; 3:1; 4:7). The slavery of trying harder, working for approval, looking down on those who fail, or being proud that you think you are better than other believers. Throughout Galatians his message is something like this: "To add law-keeping to faith in Jesus is not *another gospel, it's not a gospel at all!* It's bad news, horrible news! It's abandoning God's grace! Why go back to slavery?" Paul is just about beside himself as he points the Galatians to the freedom that comes to us only by grace through faith in Jesus *alone*. "For freedom Christ has set us free; stand firm therefore, and do not submit again to a yoke of slavery" (Galatians 5:1).

Our tendency to revert to salvation by works is aided by our determined enemy, Satan. He absolutely hates it when we live in and enjoy our freedom from condemnation, so he prowls around like a starved lion seeking to devour us by heaping on us guilt and condemnation for not measuring up to the perfection of God's law.[3] This is precisely why Paul tells us to "stand firm" and not let anyone, including ourselves, drag us to a self-salvation focused Christianity where we try to measure up to the law in order to be accepted by the Father.

Christianity is not a *do more, try harder* religion! It's a *I could never do enough, but Jesus did it all for me on the cross* relationship with your Father. This is good news for those who are weary of trying harder and doing more. But there is more.

Gospel Freedom Is *Freedom from Lusts and Addictions*

When we come to Christ in faith, we are still attacked and often feel controlled by powerful lusts and addictions. If people around us could read our thoughts and know the internal battles, they would be shocked. Our post-conversion draw to sin shocks us too! But here too the gospel provides the way for the freedom we want and need. As we focus on the Father's mercy and grace in Christ, as we remember that our sins are forgiven and eternal life is ours right now, we are gradually freed from the addictive, controlling, relationship-destroying power of sin. How does this happen? Proximity to God's holiness and power changes us as we abide with Christ (John 15:4–5). Our growing awareness and acceptance that we are truly and completely loved by God builds in us gratitude and deep love for him, which in turn pushes out our desire to sin against his love. His Spirit in us graciously, gradually, but persistently bears godly fruit in us and leads us to resist our own human passions and desires to sin (Galatians 5: 18–24).

Without Christ, we are doomed to be wild, instead of free. You name it—we can turn anything we put at the center of our lives, good or bad, into an idol. It's amazing how what we desire instead of God soon develops a life of its own—hooking us, addicting us, drawing us in farther and farther down, and deeper and deeper into self-destruction. We imagine that our desires will be satisfied. That we will have fun. That true life awaits. But the opposite is always true: Sin separates us from God, from ourselves, and from others. Sin turns us into slaves who cannot help themselves.

As a young Christian in college, I first realized my need to be released from slavery when I was driving to a Bible study and someone cut me off in traffic. Instantly enraged, I gave him "the finger" out the window and yelled an expletive in the general direction of the offending driver. All this on my way to a Bible study. The Holy Spirit being who he is (the One who comes alongside to help, convict, and teach) and where he is (inside me) used that as a teaching opportunity. Of course, this wasn't the first time I had been that angry. But this was the time that the Spirit opened my eyes to a pattern of anger out of control.

Shaken, after the study I told my college-career pastor about what happened as I was on the way to talk about Jesus. With a smile he recommended I read, no *memorize*, Romans 6. "The whole chapter?!" "Yes, the whole chapter." It was life-changing for me to meditate on Romans 6. I learned that what Jesus accomplished for me on the cross meant I was no longer a slave to behavior that he hated and I hated too. Because of Jesus, I was no longer a slave to the anger that was controlling me and killing my relationships. Of course, this applies not only to my anger issues, but to every area of sin I've wrestled with in life.

Every man deals with lust. I remember the first time I said while preaching that "every man deals with sexual temptation." A friend told me I got him in trouble because on the way home from church his wife asked, "Do you struggle with sexual temptation?" Of course he had to honestly answer yes. I was glad because she needed to know, and he needed to tell her. We live in a sex-crazed world where sexual images are literally everywhere. What man could not be tempted?

Addiction to pornography is so pervasive among men and young men in particular that it's arguably the number one "brick wall" keeping boys from becoming real men. One astounding statistic asserts that "68 percent of

Christian men and 50 percent of pastors view pornography regularly."[4] I am not saying this to be condemning or discouraging, but we have to face the truth. Sexual addiction is a deal-breaker for biblical manhood in that it stunts our growth and keeps us in a guilt and shame cycle that makes being the Father's sons almost out of the question. After one of my talks on the destructive power of pornography, a man wrote to me anonymously.

> Oh, it's dynamite, alright. And it can detonate your life, your soul, if you're not careful. I share a portion of my story so that maybe other men and their families may benefit from it. Until recently I was living in the hell that is pornography. Every chance I had at home, when my wife and two kids were asleep, I would sneak into my office, lock the door, and fire up the computer. This depravity went on so long that, over time, I had very little interest in my wife sexually, seeing only her imperfections. The distance that widened between us grew until I began to see anything she said or did, even for my benefit, as a mere annoyance. And I drank—out of shame. Finally, not too long ago, I hit bottom. No, I didn't get caught. I didn't lose my job or anything like that. I just became so disgusted with myself that I just couldn't take it anymore. I hated everything, including myself.

I hope and pray that he didn't stay stuck in sin and self-hatred. The gospel call for him (and all others caught in sin) is to go by faith to Jesus and ask for forgiveness. When you fail, ask for forgiveness again (1 John 1:9–10). Then, by faith, keep on believing in the forgiveness of sins that Jesus purchased for you on the cross.

If pornography is your issue, get and read *Samson and the Pirate Monks: Calling Men to Authentic Brotherhood* by Nate Larkin. You'll be drawn to authenticity and freedom and it'll change your life. Jesus sets us free from sin. He sets us free from all the false gods we think will fill the emptiness inside. That's gospel freedom for us, but there's more.

Gospel Freedom Is *Freedom from People-Pleasing*

Some Christians heap guilt on us mercilessly with a non-biblical, conscience-binding morality. They love us and have a wonderful plan for our lives. I understand this well because I'm a pastor and have learned from the best of them. I saw a bumper sticker once that said, "My mother is a travel agent for guilt trips." But of course moms get a bad rap. We can all put others under the law of our own rules, roles, and expectations. And we can all feel the weight of those things in our relationships. But grace frees us the people-pleasing that drives us to fake a persona or wear masks that hide the real us.

When you understand the cross and the grace you received there, then you know that there is nothing to add to what Jesus has accomplished. And you know that it is more important to listen to the voice of your Savior leading you by his Spirit than trying to please everyone in your life (who will always have an opinion about what you should be doing and when). Jesus had unlimited patience with sinners, but no patience at all for the religious elite who stopped by to give him directions about who he should eat and drink with and what he should do and not do on the Sabbath (Matthew 11:18–19; 12:1–14). Steve Brown often says that when it comes to Christian freedom "you should live your life with such freedom that uptight Christians will doubt your salvation."

Here's what Fenelon wrote about living in freedom from others' agenda for him: "I am a blessedly free man, and I try to do each day whatever I feel the Lord is leading me to do. Of course, those who are trying to figure out where I will be and when are sadly mixed up. God bless them! I am not trying to annoy them, but I insist on freedom in the Lord."[5] As sons of the living God free in Christ, we too can "insist" on our freedom. That's gospel freedom, but still we're not quite done.

Gospel Freedom Is *Freedom for Radical Love and Sacrificial Serving*

We are freed by Jesus not so that we will go back to being wild and doing whatever we want, but so that we can live for the glory of God and the good of people: "Live as people who are free, not using your freedom as a cover-up for evil, but living as servants of God" (1 Peter 2:16).

Christians have a rich history in sacrificial living and dying because of the life-giving reality of the gospel.

The book of Acts shows how gospel freedom energized Jesus's disciples to throw caution to the wind and boldly promote their risen Lord. As a young Christian, I'll never forget pouring through the page-turner *Through Gates of Splendor.*[6] The story of how Jim Elliot, Pete Fleming, Ed McCully, Nate Saint, and Roger Youderian and their courageous wives reached the Huaorani tribe of eastern Ecuador absolutely blew me away. Elliot's oft-quoted line "He is no fool to give what he cannot keep to gain what he cannot lose" has rung in my ears ever since. Those young men were free to sacrifice their lives (and did) because the gospel had set them free. The impact of their lives and deaths led to the conversion of hundreds in the Huaorani tribe and set an example that many have followed as they share Christ all over the world.

When we live out the radical freedom that we have in Christ, we serve where we are wired, gifted, and called to serve, not because we are guilted into serving. We give generously because we want to, not because we have to. Contrary to conventional Christian wisdom, gospel freedom really does unleash us to love more authentically, purely, and joyfully. We tell people about Jesus because he has set us free, and we would love to see others be free too. As we serve, we become more willing to suffer. Grace gives us freedom to give ourselves away, because Jesus gave himself away for us first.

The Triune God is free. The Father is free, and he is not content with his sons being slaves. So he does everything with the Son and Spirit to set us free. Like Father, like sons.

Take It to Heart

1. Would you say that you are "wild" or "free" following the definitions early in this chapter? What are the differences between being wild and being free? How does being wild or free shape life (2 Samuel 11—12; Psalm 51)?

2. How is your understanding of freedom different from the biblical definitions of freedom in this chapter (Romans 6; 8:1–2; Galatians 5:1–3; 1 Peter 2:16)?

3. Read again through the list of ways the gospel brings you freedom. Where do you still feel trapped in your life? How do Paul's words in Romans 7:14–25 map onto your experience? What hope does Paul end Romans 7 with?

4. Which of the aspects of freedom mentioned in the chapter do you most need today? How do you think you can grow in understanding your freedom in Christ?

5. How can a Christian man enjoy life with this view of freedom? Challenge: Explain this view of

freedom to another Christian guy and see how he responds to it.

6. How might your life change if you lived out of the freedom you have in Christ? Share with another person (or in your small group) where you see your lack of freedom. Ask for prayer and meditate and/ or memorize Romans 6 together. Make a commitment to check in with each other regularly.

7

The Adventuring Father

"The very basic core of a man's living spirit
is his passion for adventure."[1]
Christopher McCandless

Life is either a daring adventure or nothing.
Security does not exist in nature, nor do the children
of men as a whole experience it. Avoiding danger is
no safer in the long run than exposure.[2]
Helen Keller

Teddy Roosevelt was on an adventure and things were
going badly—so badly that he decided the only way out
was suicide. For two months the former president of the
United States had been deep in the Brazilian jungle, a
month of it already spent on a tortuous and an uncharted
tributary of the Amazon River aptly named the River
of Doubt. Already struggling with malaria and dysen-
tery, Teddy was further weakened when the expedition's
canoes swamped—trapped in vines near vicious white
water and an upcoming waterfall. Rushing into the swift
current, Roosevelt helped free the dugouts, but on the
way back to the shore slipped and the force of the current

slammed his leg into a sharp rock. As he limped to the shore, blood was already spurting out of the wound. In the Amazon rain forest, surrounded by bacteria and parasites, his injury was life-threatening.[3]

Colonel Rondon, the expedition leader, after scouting the upcoming falls, said it was impossible to portage the canoes around the falls and they would have to walk out of the jungle. By the next night it was obvious that Roosevelt's leg was infected and his malaria was back. After a night of suffering, Teddy called a morning pow-wow with his friend, naturalist George Cherrie, and Teddy's son Kermit and said, "Boys, I realize that some of us are not going to finish this journey. Cherrie, I want you and Kermit to go on. You can get out. I will stop here."[4] Kermit would have none of it, and was in such despair that Roosevelt knew that to save his son, he would have to make it out of the jungle with him. They did make it out together, and the story of how Roosevelt and his party explored and survived the River of Doubt is one of the most astounding true-to-life adventures ever undertaken.

But what are we to think of Teddy's excellent and dangerous adventure? Certainly Teddy Roosevelt was a man who lived on the cutting edge of adventure and excitement, most of it of his own making. Having gone down in defeat in the presidential elections of 1912, *The Independent*, a Kansas City newspaper, was surely on target when it reported that "Roosevelt's frantic desire to make an impact in his final years by making his mark on the map of the Western Hemisphere almost cost him, his son, and his team their lives."[5]

"Roosevelt's frantic desire to make an impact" are words which haunt me. He was a man driven to make and leave his mark—to prove, to find, to create an identity, and to overcome the shame at disappointing his supporters due to his recent loss. He needed public human approval like a starving shark needs a fish. Adventure was a way to be distracted from the pain of his public failure, while at the same time a means to the end of building the identity of a successful man. Roosevelt was looking for life through his adventures. Many men today are doing the same thing with risky behavior, a grand plan to make a mark, the desire to find identity in accomplishments—they all fuel our love for adventure. And sometimes, like Roosevelt, we don't care who might get hurt along the way.

Defining Life as a Gift and an Adventure

Roosevelt defined "life" as great deeds done in the public eye. Take a moment and think about how you define life. We live life, but can we define what it is? We all have a definition, even if it's subconscious, and it affects what we do every day. Your definition of life affects your family, your coworkers, how you use your time, possessions, and talents. Some of us define life negatively—something to be endured. Others of us define life positively—an adventure to be embraced, to get the most out of. But why not go to the Creator of life for his definition? Our heavenly Father teaches us in his Word that life is a gift to be enjoyed and an adventure to go on with Jesus (Genesis 1:31; Psalm 73:25–28; Matthew 4:18–22; Acts 5:41–42).

Each of us has been given life as a gift from God. We didn't choose to be created and placed here on earth. God chose us and every breath we take is a gift from him. God meant for us to enjoy him and everything he created. That was the original plan for Adam and Eve in the garden. God looked at what he made, said it was good, and gave Adam and Eve the job of being in charge of everything. What an adventure that would have been—supervising God's perfect creation and filling the earth with people who loved God and loved each other! Of course, we can only imagine that adventure because when Adam and Eve disobeyed God in the garden, life became broken and hard.

But all was not lost. Immediately after the fall, even in the midst of cursing his creation, God promised our redemption, intending to restore our relationship with him (Genesis 3:15). So the Father sent his Son, and what Jesus accomplished in his visible earthly work as the incarnated Son of God was redemption. In the work of Jesus Christ, the curse is lifted from those who put their trust in him as Redeemer and Lord. Life as a free gift and an adventure is restored.

As we saw in the last chapter, although we are born to be wild, we were originally created to be free. When we put our faith in Jesus, our freedom is restored, and now, as sons of God and Jesus's brothers, we follow him into the greatest adventure of all—bringing his kingdom of love, justice, and righteousness to this broken world. Being part of God's kingdom coming and his will being done is more exciting, challenging, hair-raising, and fulfilling than any adventure we could think of. This is an adventure where we follow Jesus in the biggest adventure of all—giving up what we want to do naturally and putting ourselves at the service of others. That's a life-changing adventure!

When John the Baptist began his ministry, his message was simple, "Repent for the kingdom of heaven is at hand." Jesus had the same message, "Repent, for the kingdom of heaven is at hand" (Matthew 3:2; 4:17). Jesus was telling people that a crucial moment had arrived in history—God had arrived in their midst. Restoration had begun. He was on a mission to bring God's kingdom to earth.

In the life, death, and resurrection of our Lord Jesus, we have all that is necessary for us to enter into the kingdom of God. The perfect life of love that is impossible for us to accomplish has been lived for us by Jesus. The debt we owe to God for going our own way has been paid for us by Jesus's death. The power to live a new life of love is ours through the Spirit. Jesus laid down his life for us that we might live. Now he calls all of his followers to go with him on the greatest adventure of all—laying down their lives for others so they might know Jesus and live as well (Matthew 28:19). We are called to join with him in spreading the good news that God has come and that reconciliation with the Father is possible.

Danger in the Adventure

Yes, there is great danger involved in following Jesus. Ultimate victory is assured because a tomb is empty in Jerusalem. One day evil will be done away with forever, the earth will be restored, and we will have new adventures with God that we can only imagine. Until then King Jesus is leading his followers on the grand and dangerous adventure of reclaiming the world for himself. It's dangerous because the same forces of evil—within and without—that sent Jesus to die a cruel death are still at work in our world. Men and women do not want to give up their right to go their own way, even as they go toward death and destruction forever. The prince of this world—Satan—does not want people to live and follow Jesus and he will try any means to stop God's kingdom from coming. We live in a bad and broken world where those of us who are called to tell people the good news of the King and his kingdom find it dangerous to do so.

Spreading the good news of the kingdom can be exciting and exhilarating as we see people trust Jesus and experience freedom from guilt and shame. The gospel gives hope to the hopeless and comfort to sinners and sufferers. But it's dangerous work we do as Christians because we have enemies. Jesus's successful combat with Satan shows us that the most dangerous enemies he and his people have are invisible and shadowy (Matthew 4:1–11).

It was right after Jesus's temptation in the wilderness that he called his disciples to go on a kingdom adventure with him: "Follow me, and I will make you fishers of men" (Matthew 4:18–22). They followed him by the power of his Spirit into a war—the greatest war ever waged. New Testament scholar William Hendriksen explains it like this:

> . . . the Son of God was going forth to war. He was destroying the works of the devil, teaching and preaching, casting out demons and healing sickness by the power of the Spirit, thus healing both soul and body, and more and more establishing the kingdom of God on earth (Matthew 12:28).[6]

The apostle Paul describes the Christian adventure as a spiritual war (Ephesians 6:10–20), and though war is often scary, it's seldom boring. A lot of us are a bit bored, aren't we? But that is only because we don't realize what a grand adventure we have been called to participate in with Jesus. We live in a time of kingdom advancement and fruit-bearing adventure. Jesus has called us to go with him to the world and to bear much fruit (John 15:1–5). Without him we can do nothing, but with him, and in him, life is a great adventure where what we do in Jesus's name bears fruit for eternity. It's time for Christian men to realize that we were created for bold work and great adventures as God the Father's beloved sons, with Jesus as our Lord, leader, and elder brother, and the Spirit as our power source.

We are completely loved and unconditionally accepted in Christ. God loves me more than I could ever know. At the same time, my life is not my own. I am expendable and can be used by my loving Father in any way he chooses. The combination of being a deeply loved and an expendable son taps into our manhood as the Father made us. We were made to live, fight, and possibly die for something very important. Being noticed or successful isn't what will give our life meaning. But to expend ourselves so that God's kingdom will come and his will be done? That's an adventure worth living and dying for.

Dietrich Bonhoeffer was one of the most courageous Christian men of his time. Raised in a wealthy, educated, and influential family in the post-WWI era, Bonhoeffer became a German theologian and pastor committed to the gospel in a time when many of his intellectual pedigree and position were abandoning true faith. Deeply committed to Christ, his people, and his kingdom, Bonhoeffer preached about his Lord and what faithfulness to Jesus meant in a time when Hitler's Nazi regime was wreaking havoc—killing Jews, toppling governments, and shedding blood all over Europe and North Africa.

In the midst of this turmoil, Bonhoeffer taught that the grace of God in Christ is an extravagant gift that

God's children should respond to with service and sacrifice. Bonhoeffer was glad to live for Christ, and he was also glad to die for him. Imagine this scene from prison in the words of Bonhoeffer's friend Payne Best:

> He had hardly finished his last prayer when the door opened and two evil-looking men in civilian clothes came in and said: "Prisoner Bonhoeffer. Get ready to come with us." Those words "Come with us"—for all prisoners they had come to mean one thing only—the scaffold. We bade him good-bye—he drew me aside—"This is the end," he said. "For me the beginning of life."[7]

There is danger in the great adventure of following Jesus, sometimes even death. For the Christian, however, death is the beginning of life.

Mapping Your Adventure at Work

Our heavenly Father intends adventure to be an everyday experience, not just something saved for the weekend or summer vacation. When God made Adam and Eve, he gave them the job (and adventure) of having dominion over the whole earth (Genesis 1:26). Work was not a burden, but a joy and a part of what it meant to be made in the image of God. But after the fall, work became a struggle. If you have to do the same thing day after day, where is the adventure in that? Or if your work is demanding, demeaning, and low-paying, where is the adventure in that? But, in Christ, our everyday work is redeemed and transformed. We work hard because it is the Lord Christ we are serving (Colossians 3:24). Why? Because our ultimate goal is not to get ahead in this life, but to be a part of God's kingdom coming and his will being done. That's our calling and our adventure.

Every day, as Christ followers, we go to work to provide for ourselves, our family, and to help those in need (2 Thessalonians 3:11–13; Ephesians 4:28). But we also have the unique call to bring heaven to earth, to "make disciples of all nations" as we work. When Jesus comes again, the whole earth will be made new and whole. But until then, through our work, we get to be the Father's hands and feet as we now live our creational purpose by following Jesus and building his kingdom here on earth.

There are different ways of participating with Jesus in his kingdom work—as many different ways as there are people. When men find and use their spiritual gifts and start seeing God work through them, it launches them into a whole new adventure. As we saw earlier, the Father loves to empower us to bear much fruit. As we bear fruit, we bring glory to God and blessing to others. Those are the things we do that last for eternity. That's the way to make a lasting impact on this world.

The opportunity to be used in the lives of others as a servant and conduit of God's grace is a greater and more fulfilling adventure than any monument you could build on earth. I am reminded of this every time I see someone pour his life out for others. My friend Alan Gooch, a former assistant football coach at the University of Central Florida, has had a vision for the past seven years to bring a college football playoff bowl to Orlando that will help raise significant funding for cancer research. The "Cure Bowl" has been a boatload of work, along with a lot of disappointments, dashed hopes, and redirections, but it's finally going to happen. When Alan gets to attend the Cure Bowl, you can be sure that all the hard work will be worth it. His adventure isn't about getting himself noticed or becoming famous, it's all about helping others because he loves Jesus. That's the kind of adventure worth our blood, sweat, and tears!

Mapping Your Adventure in Relationships

It sometimes astonishes people when I say that men really are pretty relational. Are we task oriented? Of course. Do we pursue relationships in the same way women do? Hardly ever. Do we isolate ourselves, wear masks, and deny that we need other people? All too often true. Nevertheless, we do consciously want a few good relationships, and guys, we have to recognize that a good bit of the adventure the Father calls us into has to do with people. Even if we never get married and have kids, we are still called into community with others. When asked for a bottom-line summation of Old Testament law, Jesus uttered these words, "You shall love the Lord your

God with all your heart and with all your soul and with all your mind. This is the great and first commandment. And a second is like it: You shall love your neighbor as yourself" (Matthew 22:37–39). Relationship with God and others is the basic reality and blessing of life.

An elder at our church used to joke about how men tend to "use" other people. He often said, "I have friends I haven't even used yet!" Okay, we're guilty as charged. We can deceive ourselves that we are being kind and willing to serve others at church or in our network, when in reality we're looking at them as a business contact or a future sale. But that's not the gospel way, is it? Nor is it the way to a rich, fulfilling life. Instead, Jesus calls us to "deny yourself and follow me." It's the best way to live and the only way to make relationships work!

Part of the adventure in relationships is intentionally forming friendships with other guys. It's easy for men to be "bucks"—men who hide from others and don't want to risk being known and getting to know others. But we grow in community. We need other men to talk with, pray with, and to be accountable to. As I have worked with men all over the country, I have seen how we change to be like Christ as we live in community together. The Father doesn't have just one son. He has many sons, and he intends for them to be brothers together—brothers who share their joys, sorrows, sins, and service.

During my internship at Briarwood Presbyterian Church years ago under Dr. Frank Barker, stories abounded about how Dr. Barker, the senior pastor of a large church, would serve people in surprising ways. Feeding someone's dog while they were away on vacation was just one of them. Are you kidding me! What he did smelled like Jesus. Do you want to experience some incredible adventures? Serve someone who cannot pay you back, even in small ways. James said it with a punch, "Religion that is pure and undefiled before God, the Father, is this: to visit orphans and widows in their affliction, and to keep oneself unstained from the world" (James 1:27).

The Marriage Adventure

What other relationship adventures are there? For many men, one of the biggest challenges (and adventures) will be their marriage. As G. K. Chesterton purportedly joked, "Marriage is an adventure, like going to war." I was ten when my parents divorced and there weren't many kids in my category at church—a child from a divorced couple. Since then divorce has affected countless families. Now millions of men, women, and children have been torn apart by divorce. Amazingly, people are still getting married! We haven't given up on marriage even though it looks more like "serial monogamy."

Remember, adventure involves excitement, danger, *and* self-sacrifice—all of which are part of marriage. Adventures always have a gripping upside. They break the routine, provide new goals, draw out creativity, sharpen thinking, bring people together, stretch and transform, and they are sometimes physically challenging.

Adventures always have a compelling downside as well. We have to sacrifice our desires, wants, and needs for the good of someone. That is always difficult, unnatural, complicated, and exhausting. But just because there is a downside to an adventure doesn't mean you bail on it. The marriage adventure has to draw continually on the resources of grace so we can repent of our own failures to love well, and then get up and move right back into the relationship. The great adventure of following Jesus Christ in marriage can bring deep satisfaction as you faithfully love your wife over decades.

The Father is so good in clarifying to us, his sons, how a marriage relationship ought to work, since so many of us did not have any cogent explanation or consistent model. For many, marriage seems something that is just done, or to be endured, or to be exchanged when good feelings go bad. But God's purpose for marriage is for a man and woman to become one flesh (Genesis 2:24). To become "one flesh" takes a marriage ceremony and a lifetime. I like to joke when I speak on marriage that Caron and I have been married for thirty-six years, the very best years of her life! She, of course, rolls her eyes because the truth is it has been the best years of our life together. Certainly it's an adventure that I am blessed to be on with her.

I can't tell you how much I've learned about myself, people, children, life, and God from my wife. It's been an adventure of learning to love someone other than myself—listening, problem solving, growing, asking for forgiveness, sharing life's burdens, and learning to lead through service and sacrifice.

The apostle Paul teaches men that there is danger and excitement in the adventure of loving our wives "as Christ loved the church and gave himself up for her" (Ephesians 5:25). The excitement comes as we learn to lead and love sacrificially, while at the same time there is perceived danger in denying ourselves. In every adventure there ought to be some mystery, and there is mystery in marriage for sure (Ephesians 5:32), but what a profound joy to grow daily to love our wives as we naturally love ourselves (Ephesians 5:33). If you're called to marriage, it's definitely an ongoing learning and growing adventure.

It's true that some adventures come apart and some marriages do too. Maybe yours did. If you've been through divorce, you need to know that my purpose here is not to heap guilt for a broken marriage on your bruised ego, battered soul, and bleeding family. Divorce is incredibly painful. It's the death of a relationship, with lifelong emotional downsides for everyone involved. As a pastor I've seen too many marriages detonate into a million pieces. My goal is to help you view marriage differently, as an incredibly difficult and rewarding adventure that demands the best of your manhood and the best of God's infinite grace to make it through.

Recently I met a man whose wife of many years died of cancer. They had a great marriage, and three years later he was still grieving. He felt guilty that he was still so torn up even "though it's been three years." I said, "Only three years? Keep grieving, man. What you're feeling is what you're supposed to feel. When your soul is ripped in half you will feel it for a long, long time, possibly until you meet her again in heaven." His deep grief was because he had gotten what marriage was all about. He was "all in" with this wife, just as his heavenly Father was "all in" with him. His grief was good.

The Fathering Adventure

When you are fathered by *the* Father, you are fathered well and then you can pass on the good stuff you've received to your kids. I absolutely love being a dad. My family (now grown with two daughters-in-law added) has made me a rich man. I wouldn't exchange the adventure of working with my wife to raise our children for anything. My friend Pat Morley, who teaches with Man in the Mirror, often says that "no amount of success at work can ever compensate for failure at home." When I was a church planter hustling to start a church, one of the older men in our core group would regularly ask me, "Pete, are you spending enough time with your family?" Later I realized that he didn't have a close relationship with his children because he had ignored them while they were young.

My kids aren't perfect, and they won't be until they see Jesus face-to-face, but my heavenly Father has called me to be their dad—and to hang in there with them just the way he hangs in there with me. The love of the Father has done something amazing in our home. He has made me a faithful dad. That wasn't my life experience growing up, but in Christ we are not doomed to repeat the mistakes of our dads. God can (and does) do something new.

There is a new thing in the Alwinson family—a dad that hangs in there through all of the adventures of parenting. Raising kids is an adventure that the Father uses to develop us as men at the same time we are helping our kids develop, and it gives us great joy. The adventure of sacrificial fathering begins right at birth when the welcoming of a totally dependent, fragile newborn rocks the new mom and dad's world. Sleep deprivation, unfamiliar noises, and never-ending messy new jobs conspire with inexperience to keep parents off-balance. I'm told the same is true for those who joyfully bring home an adopted child. A new father begins to learn the crucial importance of self-denial and sacrifice for the good of their child on day one. Hopefully a man realizes quickly that it's impossible for a new mother to care for the baby alone and that he must be integrally involved! It's only the beginning, however. For years a father has the privilege of nurturing and developing his children, and the task grows in importance during the years.

In the Old Testament God assigned to the father (and of course mothers too) the role of passing on the faith of Israel to his children, and this idea is carried over into the father role in the New Testament (Ephesians 6:4). Dads are responsible to teach the most important things about life to their children. That includes knowing who God is and therefore who they are (identity), and teaching children to love God as creator, provider, and redeemer (Deuteronomy 6:4–9).

We get to teach our children on the way at different times during the day (Deuteronomy 6:7–9). What an adventure it is to teach our kids how Jesus's life, death, and resurrection fulfilled God's promise to bring redemption to the world. Yes, we're called to be Bible teachers, interpreters, and theologians in our children's lives, while seeking to build into them character that fits and follows the gospel. All this without being heavy-handed and discouraging! "Fathers, do not provoke your children, lest they become discouraged" is a challenge for every one of us (Colossians 3:21). This is how our heavenly Father relates to us. So, of course, like Father, like son.

When we see being a father as a grace adventure, we are inspired to provide just the right amount of structure needed in a home, to analyze and interact with our wives as to how we're doing as parents, and to listen and learn from each other in giving direction and instruction. There is adventure in learning the unique temperament and makeup of each of our children, and teaching and disciplining them with skill as individuals.

Parenting "principles" can be learned from Scripture and other experienced parents, but there is always an art to applying those principles to each of our children. What an adventure it is to develop our sons into men and our girls into women. To challenge them to do the right and difficult things in life, rather than take the popular and easier paths, and to teach our children to prepare for the tough times in life and even to suffer for Jesus is part of the adventure of fathering. One of my favorite stories of fathering comes from pastor and author Erwin McManus: "Not long ago Aaron [his son] asked me, 'Dad, would you purposefully put us in danger?' 'Yes,' I answered, 'of course.' Without blinking an eye his response was simply, 'That's what I thought. I was just making sure.'"[8] A father must teach his sons and daughters a faith-based toughness that is willing to suffer and deal with danger. It's part of the adventure of fathering that is taught us by the Father. Like Father, like son.

You Are Not on Adventure Alone

In the movie *The Kingdom of Heaven* there is a motto the blacksmith lives by, "He is no man who does not make the world a better place." That is the adventure God is calling you to. God wants you to bring heaven to earth through your work, your relationships, your marriage, and your fathering. But don't forget that you are not going on this adventure by yourself and in your own strength. Andrew Murray put it well when he said, "Jesus's call was always: Come to me and stay with me."[9] Staying with Jesus is another way of abiding in Christ and living out of the joy of his presence. As you do this, the Spirit of Christ upholds you and helps you no matter what God calls you to.

You can only go on this grand adventure as you abide in Christ. Every day is an adventure when a man, transformed by God's grace, gets up, wipes the sleep out of his eyes and the fog out of his mind, and says, "Alright Father, what are we going to do together today?" An adventuring father develops adventuring sons who can look at each new day as an adventure! Like Father, like son.

Take It to Heart

1. What is one of your greatest life adventures? If you're using this in a group, talk for several minutes about your favorite adventures and why you enjoyed them so much. Are you an adventure-loving man? Why? Why not?

2. How does life as an adventure that God calls you to differ from your view of adventure? Describe one of your kingdom adventures.

3. Why is it so important to depend on Christ and his armor as you go on a kingdom adventure (Matthew 4:1–11; Ephesians 6:10–20)?

4. This chapter maps the adventure for a man. Which area is the most difficult adventure for you to enter and why (Matthew 22:37–39; Ephesians 4:28; 2 Thessalonians 3:11–13)? How could you gain insight and expertise in that area? Who could you call this week to talk with about it?

5. If married, how can you focus on marriage more as an adventure (Genesis 2:24; Ephesians 5:25)? How can the different seasons of marriage be opportunities for adventure in marriage?

6. For dads, how can you see fathering during the different stages of your children's life as an adventure (Colossians 3:21)? How can having a close relationship with a small group of fathers help in the adventure of developing your children through the many phases of their lives? A challenge: Build a core of fathers who can help each other in the adventure of fathering.

8

The Guiding Father

"God is not in the business
of keeping his will from us!"[1]

Steve Brown

In one of the coldest winters on record in Argentina, before dawn, six Americans fully geared up in camouflage tumbled out of a packed minivan. Wiping sleep from our eyes and downing the last of our coffee, we grabbed our shotguns and shells, pulled up our waders, and dutifully followed our guides into the ice-encrusted water to the place they had selected for us to wait for sunup, when the duck hunting would begin.

A few minutes before sunrise, we could hear and see the duck's shadowy movement and then ducks on the move! I'm not going to lie—I missed way more than I took as prizes, and on that morning my fingers simply were too numb to discern that I had tried to insert a 12-gauge round in backwards. It got stuck, and I needed a younger man, my son, to get it out and get me back in the hunt. But it was still the greatest duck-hunting adventure I've ever been on. I have a picture of my son and

I struggling to hold up two armfuls of ducks. Here's the truth of that adventure: we couldn't have done it without a guide.

Like most guys, I like to do everything myself. I'd rather not have a guide or ask for directions. That's the typical man code, and I'm pretty consistent about that approach to life. Except when

1. I don't know where I am or where I am going.
2. I have a lot on the line.
3. I want to get the biggest bang for my buck (or in this case, duck) and be a success.

Only then, in those extreme conditions, do I desire and even demand a guide. When I *clearly and obviously* am out of my element and want to experience a great adventure and be a success at it, then I am astonishingly open to getting input from another person. I will even pay for a friendly guide to help me out. Why face the absolutely unknown alone? Do I look like an idiot?

Our Father-Guide

Of course, the older I get, the more I realize that my three conditions for needing a guide are true every day of my life. Every day of our lives we navigate and travel in dangerous and uncharted territories, where we need help and direction. When you think about, none of us have the infinite knowledge and wisdom that is needed to guide ourselves.

But our heavenly Father does. God created us, sent his Son to redeem us, and then sent his Spirit to fill us because he wants to be involved in our lives. That's what good fathers do. They don't just procreate kids. They delight in their children, want to do life with them, and guide them into wholeness and happiness.

All through the Bible, God the Father reassures his people that he is their ever-present, faithful guide. In the Old Testament we read that the Lord leads, restores, and walks with us through the valley of the shadow of death (Psalm 23). God also promises that he will counsel us, keep his eye on us, guide us, and make our paths straight (Psalm 32:8; 73:24; Proverbs 3:5–6). The New Testament adds the even richer theme of sonship—now, in Christ, we are firstborn heirs of the living God. We are his sons (Galatians 4:4–7). Our heavenly Father promises that his Spirit will live in our hearts and guide us into "all truth" (John 16:13).

That's why I think of myself as *God's boy*. The gospel—the good news—is that in Jesus I am now a child of God (John 1:12). Even though I'm a grown man, I'm not supposed to figure out my life without a father to guide me. Because of Jesus I don't have to. In Christ I am welcomed into his family. God is now my Father.

Sons need to hear from their father often. They need to have someone who is available to them to answer the millions of questions growing boys have through life's phases. We men need a Father we can completely trust—one who is always available to help us make sense of our world and our calling as men. We can learn a lot from others, but there is no replacement for a dad. And because of the gospel, we have one, God the Father, the Ancient of Days, our Abba, who loves to build his boys.

The Father has always guided his children in his way and his time, but he does lead us. He will not be denied. The Father's loving, reassuring, and firm voice of guidance can be heard as he speaks to us through his Spirit.

Jesus, after teaching his disciples the flow of prayer and what topics should mark our prayer to the Father (Luke 11:1–4), then challenges and commands his disciples to boldly ask God because he is a good father and good fathers provide for their children (Luke 11:5–13). His closing line is this, "If you then, who are evil, know how to give good gifts to your children, how much more will the heavenly Father give the Holy Spirit to those who ask him!"(Luke 11:13). The Father who guided us to salvation guides us as his sons by the supreme gift of the Holy Spirit every day. The Spirit speaks truth, encouragement, conviction, and direction to us through the Bible, through other believers, and sometimes just in the quiet of our own hearts.

The Father Speaks Real Truth to Real People

The hunting guides I know tend to be strong silent types who ration out words like water in the desert—they speak so low and so seldom that you have to strain to hear what they're telling you to do. It's easy to think that God is like that—a strong silent type who looks right through us and really doesn't want to talk much, let alone to us. Perhaps your father was like that as well. But our heavenly Father is not like that. He wants to talk to his sons. He is "all in" with his children every moment of every day. And he has given us the Bible, a large book filled with his words of comfort, hope, help, conviction, and instruction.

I've read the Bible and have been a Bible student and teacher for more than thirty-five years, and I still need to be mastered by God's words to me every day. You can spend a lifetime reading our Father's words to us (like me), but you won't get to the end of your need to hear from him. In every situation, every relationship, and every season on life, God's words come to us to guide us and help us. Whatever you are struggling with right now, be assured that God wants to speak to you through his Word, to help you grow in your trust and love for him. He wants to help you love others too. But you have to pick up your Bible and listen to your guide! When you do, you will find that your Father is speaking directly to you.

I'm desperate to hear my Father's voice every day so this is what I do—I make an appointment with him every day. I call it my daily appointment with God (DAWG), and it's the first thing on my morning calendar. My day begins like this: get up, throw on some clothes, start the coffee, ask my Father for a mind to understand and a heart to hear him speak to me, and then read a Psalm and a chapter in Proverbs (there are thirty-one chapters), reflect on what I read, and write down a couple of key thoughts that stood out to me.

As I read the Psalms, I see God exalted, so my view of God is raised and I can exalt him too. Proverbs give wisdom for living a Godward life, and invariably one of the lines of Proverbs is highlighted for me by the Spirit for that day's appointments or projects. By the time I'm into my third cup coffee, I'm ready to dip into a Gospel to hear and soak in my Lord's words. Usually I start by repenting for the bad news in my life (my sin) and then I go on to remember the good news—Christ's work on my behalf—so the Father can reset my identity as his son, not as a worker or leader or one of the other roles or callings in my life. When I finish a Gospel, I'll go next to one of the letters in the New Testament and read slowly for several days through it.

How much time does this take? I started out with about ten or fifteen minutes, but it has grown because quite frankly the most enjoyable part of my day is spending time with my Father. I've found myself going to bed earlier and getting up earlier so I can get more face time with him. He's never failed to show up, though sometimes it takes me a while to wake up and sense his presence.

Over time, working through books of the Bible in a steady way every day or several days a week, it's amazing how the Father's sons can come to hear his whisper as clear if it were a shout. Because you're his son and his Spirit is in you, you can understand what God said to his people in history and how that applies to you today. As you hear God's voice to you, inevitably you'll want to study the Bible even more. The different types of literature in the Bible such as historical narrative, poetry, wisdom literature, and letters will intrigue you and you'll want to understand how God is speaking to his children through them. I challenge you to make a daily appointment with God and see how you're transformed over the course of a month.

As you read through your Bible, you will find the real story of God and his real people, a history that unfolds through thousands of years. That history doesn't hide the ugliness and the mistakes of God's people. Just in the first book of the Bible we encounter murder (Genesis 4), incest (Genesis 19), rape (Genesis 34), and prostitution (Genesis 38). The stories are shocking, but what is even more surprising is that God would want anything at all to do with those people. And of course, we fit right in with them, don't we? Amazingly, astonishingly, God never gives up on his chosen ones, rescuing them from Egypt and giving them world-changing, civilization-changing truth to live by. God's words in the Bible are meant for real people, living in a messed-up world, who are themselves messing up and needing daily grace and help.

Over and over again I've found God's guidance in his Word to be real-world practical truth. But it's not advice; it's God's guidance. Someone said that "when we ask for advice we are usually looking for an accomplice," and that is often true, isn't it? Usually we just want someone to say yes to a direction we already want to go in. But our all-wise, all-loving heavenly Father is never going to join us in foolish, misguided schemes we might concoct. He'd rather lead us on great adventures in the real world.

God loves to talk to his people. He has done so in the past and continues to do so in the present. In eternity we'll have so many incredible conversations that it will blow our mind. A father who never talks to his boys or answers his children when they talk to him is admittedly infuriating. That's not our God. Like any good guide the Father guides his boys, sometimes by whispering, sometimes with loud encouragement, and sometimes with a thought in our heads that just won't go away.

We Speak to Our Father

Because of Jesus, the door is always open for us to go to our Father and talk things over. We don't just hear his words to us in the Bible; we can talk to our Father too, whenever we want. Prayer is simply talking with God. As the perfect Father, God wants to hear from you. That's why he tells us, even commands us, to pray all the time (1 Thessalonians 5:17). God is saying, "Talk to me. I like it and you need it."

Prayer is often difficult for men. My mentor Steve Brown says in the introduction to his book on prayer, *Approaching God*, "I have a theory: Unbelievers don't pray because they are afraid that God might be there. Believers don't pray because they are afraid that he might not be."[2] But you don't need to be afraid that your Father isn't there, and you don't have to be afraid that he is there! He is your Father who loves you, the Father who listens, who hears, who comes close in Jesus and through his Spirit. He wants to hear all about your struggles, your sins, your worries, your fears, and your dreams for the future. He is intimately involved in every part of your life.

But perhaps the reason you struggle to pray is a bit different. Maybe you think you can "make life work" on our own. That's a tendency in all of us; we don't like the feeling of being dependent, of needing help and direction. But it is in humbling ourselves before God that we receive grace (James 4:6).

For over thirty-five years as a youth pastor, church planter, and senior pastor, I have been led more times than I can count to humble myself, get on my knees, and confess to the Father that I simply did not understand what was going on with my elders or my staff, or how I should lead in a meeting the next day, or how to present a difficult pastoral situation to my congregation. Once I spent the entire night in agonizing prayer, reading Scripture and asking for clarity. Shortly after sunrise grace arrived as well. When I wake up in the middle of the night and toss and turn, it's usually because a huge issue is looming in my life and I have no answers. I've learned that sleeplessness, for me, is the cue that the Father is ready to talk and wants me quiet, humble, and ready to listen.

Following the prescription in James and realizing I don't control life and can't make it work, has made room for the Father to be the authority and strength I need. Sons who learn to humble themselves before their infinitely stronger and wiser Father are able to drink deeply of his wisdom and do find grace to help in time of need. Amazingly, but logically, the sons then have wisdom to share with others. Like Father, like son.

The Father Who Is "In Your Face"

A good father doesn't pull punches with his son. Instead of telling him that everything he is doing is great, he tells him the truth (but always in love!). Your heavenly Father's guidance is like that, but even better because your Father in heaven is perfect. Biblical guidance is often "in your face" because we need that. We need our heavenly Father to speak truth to us when we are prideful, self-centered, or just plain lazy. I enjoy David Wilkie's cartoon *Coffee with Jesus*. It's sort of Jesus "with an edge"—and just maybe the edge he would use with guys like you and me today. Take Wilkie's dialogue between landscaper Carl and Jesus about Carl's wife Lisa:

Carl: "Lisa wants me to take her to the opera, Jesus! What could suck more than that? Ugggh! The opera!"

Jesus: "Lisa hides well her hatred of football, Carl, even when you insist on watching ten hours of it on Sundays."

Carl: "Lisa hates football? But she sits there and watches with me and never complains."

Jesus: "I love watching it sink in, Carl." [3]

Sometimes those "in your face" moments come as we pray, or as we read the Bible, but often they come from others who love us—our wives, children, or friends. It might not feel like a gift in the beginning, but it will in the end. My mentor Steve Brown does that for me. One time after confessing a sin to him and telling him I was surprised at what I had done, he said, "You wouldn't be so surprised if you didn't have such a high opinion of yourself." Uh huh. Because Jesus loves me he gives me friends and family to be in my face.

Real-world guidance from our heavenly Father also is going to exclude anything that contradicts Scripture. Our Father leads and guides us through prayer, his Spirit, and godly counsel. But a son has to remember that the Father will never lead you to do something that's in clear and direct contradiction to his holy Word. So a prayer asking, *Father, please help me to figure out how to scam my customers in creative ways today. Oh, and help my income to never be discovered by the IRS!* will not be answered yes by your heavenly Father! Trust me on that.

Just-in-Time Guidance

Sometimes deadlines pass and you still don't know what to do next. You need guidance from the Father, but your time is up and you think, *what in the world am I going to do now?* Actually, your guidance for the moment is a no because it's really better not to move ahead than to move ahead without clear direction. Often the Father says to his sons, "My guidance here is this: you are not ready to make a decision now. Later. That's my guidance, son."

As I reflect on the many times I've asked our Father to do something *now,* I have to let you in on a secret—he's on a different time schedule than we are. And he's in no hurry. If anyone has tried to rush God along it's me, and doing so has always turned out to be a phenomenal waste of time. After a long life of following Jesus and trusting my Father, I'm now shocked when anything I ask for happens even remotely close to my timing. That's true with guidance as well. Almost always as we pursue God's leading about particular issues or decisions in our lives, God gives guidance at the last moment. It's just in time, just not in our time!

Richard Mouw unpacks this for us when he says, "That God sometimes works fast is a 'given' in my theology. But I have trouble with the idea that God's normal pace is fast. It's dangerous to insist that God always, or usually, operates in a quick and decisive manner."[4] Over the years I have learned this the hard way. I've spent most of my life running with the Lord instead of walking with him at his pace. As I reflect on my Father's greatness and perfection, I'm so glad he never was or ever will be frenetic like me. I'm learning to plan my work, and then let him rework my plan if need be. Now don't get me wrong, he's okay with me running and is faster than me when he wants to be.

But since our Abba is totally in control of all things, what is more important than simply keeping up with him, enjoying the conversation, his guidance, and the joy of being one of his boys? Something unique happens when a man spends many years walking with his Father and enjoying his guidance: He becomes a guide for others. Like Father, like son.

Take It to Heart

1. Who is your "go to" source for guidance in life? Who do you normally turn to for help when you need it? Do you turn to anyone besides yourself (Psalm 23)?

2. How has it worked for you in the past to "listen" to God for guidance? As you have followed Christ, has it gotten easier for you to hear his voice through the Bible, godly counselors, and circumstances (Psalms 32:8; 73:24; Proverbs 3:5–6)?

3. What did you learn in this chapter about guidance from God that can help you relate to him as a son to a Father (Luke 11:1–13)?

4. This chapter describes a method for a DAWG, a Daily Appointment With God. Does this sound like a method that you could use or adapt? Why or why not? If you're studying this book in a small group, could you all begin a DAWG and report to each other regularly about how it is going?

5. How did you respond to the section on prayer (1 Thessalonians 5:17)? Have you found connecting with the Father and getting guidance from him through prayer a benefit or a disappointment? How could a "band of brothers" help in learning to hear from the Father through prayer?

6. When you know that your heavenly Father accepts you completely because of Jesus, how can that reality enable you to take in his "in your face" feedback and guidance? How does God's grace make us less sensitive and reactionary to the Lord's leading, and more willing to accept it?

9

The Wisdom-Giving Father

"The fear of the LORD is the beginning of knowledge;
fools despise wisdom and instruction."

Proverbs 1:7

Mount Everest is the highest mountain peak in the
world. At 29,035 feet, it's a dangerous climb that claims
lives every year. In 2014 sixteen people died—the most
on record. If a climber stays in "the death zone" (above
28,000 feet) for too long, survival odds decrease dra-
matically. Even with the best preparation, sometimes
climbers just don't make it. Mount Everest is a dangerous place to work and climb. No one would dare to go
there without the proper equipment and training. To do
so would guarantee disaster.

Everest stands tall as a metaphor for life in the real
world. This world is a dangerous place. It's broken by sin
and sorrow—a true "death zone." Often we are not well
prepared for life in the death zone. If you're going to
push your limits in a world where all kinds of avalanches
can happen without notice, the very least you can do is
prepare well for the worst.

In our world today people often think that the best way to gain wisdom is to learn by experience—to make mistakes and learn from them. There is a little bit of truth in that—we shouldn't repeat the same mistakes again and again. But that's not the best strategy for entering into a dangerous situation. The stakes are too high. One mistake could mean death. You wouldn't survive long on Mount Everest if you didn't take advice from those who are wiser than you, those who know more. The same is true for the dangers we face every day—we need wisdom to guide us and protect us. The book of Proverbs is our Father's gift to us for that very purpose.

A Survival Manual for the Death Zone

Proverbs was given by the Father to equip us with the basic principles that we need to face the avalanches of life. In the first five books of the Bible, all written by Moses, we learn about creation and how God's people, the Israelites, were given a special relationship with God. As God's people, by faith, through grace, they were given many clear ways of *faith and practice*. Moses taught them principles for loving God and people and how to seek forgiveness when they failed. Proverbs takes those principles and adds even more detail. It's an up-close and personal tutorial on how to live as a restored people on a broken planet.

As a man who did not get much direction from my earthly father, Proverbs has become one of my prized possessions. Written in concise, pithy statements, Proverbs contains "man-speak" at its best. These short, distilled proverbs contain the divine wisdom you and I need to navigate through life—to learn how to love God and others in our messed-up world. Unlike the maxims of our culture, Proverbs covers the whole spectrum of our lives, all of the normal encounters we will have as well as the contingencies and unique events that we face. It's a gold mine of value to Christ-following men.

I'm on a mission for men to understand the book of Proverbs, wear the pages out, and pass it on to others. If we saturate ourselves in God's wisdom, we will benefit beyond belief. As we pass God's wisdom on to other men, they will benefit, and so will their families, churches, and even our wider world. We need more wise men in a culture where true, godly wisdom is a rare commodity.

Everyday Wisdom

When I become a Christian, I immediately wanted to know the will of God for my life. I thought something like this:

> *Okay, it's a new day. I have a Savior now, a Father, and a constant companion inside me (the Holy Spirit). I am deeply loved. The Bible says I'm even a new man. I know God redeemed me for a purpose. He has given his sons and daughters an overarching world mission, and I get to be a part*

of it! So what is my slice of the mission? I want to know what's in store for me! I want to help make it happen.

When a man is ignited by the gospel, he looks skyward for God to let down the visionary blueprint of his life. We expect our Father, the architect of the universe, to unroll the plans for our life and show us in advance what he's going to build. If we know exactly what he's trying to build, we can get with the plan and help God out. That's the way I thought. So my daily prayer became, *Lord what is it you're doing in my life? What is your will? Just tell me!* I think God smiled as I prayed.

One day I think I heard him say something like this, "So are you a contractor? Could you read the blueprints even if I gave them to you? And do you think you can decipher the complexity of my blueprints for the entire universe *and* know where you fit in?"

My reply? "Well no, but I can parse some Greek verbs and stuff."

And God said, "Stick to the verbs. Just follow me today. Let me build your life."

So my prayer "to just let me see the blueprint" changed from "just let me see it once," to "Okay, so you're never going to show it to me and you didn't ask my opinion."

What I've learned in walking with the Father is that the lion's share of God's will for our lives is given us already in the Bible. The Bible explains life and shows how God restores all of life in Christ. We are kingdom people who are mobilized to enjoy God and serve and sacrifice as he brings in his kingdom through us. This is the big picture for God's will for our lives.

In Proverbs, God gives his people the principles they need to apply in order to negotiate every conceivable situation in life. We won't get and don't need the blueprint for life. We just need the relationship with God and his everyday wisdom for dealing with life, even (and maybe especially) the unexpected, the unforeseen, the unplanned. Every day is, after all, intended to be a unique adventure.

Where Wisdom Begins

Wisdom is such a big topic. Where do we begin? Here's what we learn from Proverbs: It's quite simple. We begin with our relationship with God.

> The fear of the LORD is the beginning of knowledge; fools despise wisdom and instruction. (Proverbs 1:7)

Proverbs teaches us that wisdom begins with a healthy "fear" of God. This is not a cringing fear of punishment. The "fear of the LORD" is not a servile, docile, and flinching sense that at any time God can backhand you for messing up. When you come to Christ by faith, through God's grace, you know you are loved, forgiven, and accepted not by anything you have done, but by what

Jesus has done for you. You have been given grace, so you honor the grace Giver. This is where wisdom begins.

We know we aren't wise on our own. We couldn't even save ourselves. We know we don't have what it takes to get through life. We know we need daily help and mercy. So as God's sons who are deeply thankful for his gracious rescue, we are open to his teaching us how to live. We honor (fear) God with reverent respect and listen to him for life guidance. We know he is our only hope in our dangerous world.

When we become Christians we embark on a journey and adventure with God. As we follow Christ we want others to also be drawn to Christ. That's one reason the Father gives us such incredibly wise teaching in Proverbs, not only that we would live well, but also that others would be drawn to the originator of wisdom, God himself, who is their eternal Savior.

We Have Much to Learn (and Unlearn)

Growth in wisdom is a journey and adventure because we have so much to learn. Even though we are born again, we are still sinner-saints and sufferers in a broken world that reinforces a manhood created out of the world's wisdom rather than God's wisdom. We've spent a lot of years living and surviving in a world system that is opposed to God, so when we do come to Christ, God's way of wisdom is not instinctual to us. Instead the way the world does things is our default mode. We learn from the way we grow up and the people around us how to manage the world, but that's not God's way. It's our own version of getting ahead in life that has more to do with "street smarts" than with doing things God's way.

You might have learned to put others down to get ahead, tell only a partial truth (i.e., lie), manipulate, avoid work, use women for your pleasure, and try to get what you want in every situation to make it through life. Or you might have learned that being a success, having an important job and doing whatever it takes to keep it, is the way to success. But none of those ways of approaching life have to do with following God and becoming wise. As men changed by grace who now belong to their heavenly Father, we have to unlearn our old way of life and learn a whole new way of living.

The wisdom from Proverbs gives us a map for this new way of living—it's a map for our adventure of following Jesus. It's not a blueprint (remember God doesn't give us his plan), but instead it's the principles we need for every type of situation we will encounter. Proverbs teaches us by saying *normally this is how life works. Normally this is what you are supposed to do in the adventure of being God's covenant son.* These are principles that will stand the test of time and be for every season of your life.

I like how the guys at Iron Sharpens Iron describe the phases of a man's life: emerging men (13–19), pioneering men (20–29), full-throttle men (30–55), and seasoned men (56+). Wherever you are on that continuum, God's wisdom will guide you. Proverbs is the Father sharing his heart with his children and saying, *Alright, now I'm going to tell you how to build the best life in a broken world. Ready? Let's go.* Every man should have a father who teaches them how to live well. Because we are in Christ, we have such a father. Proverbs is his heart for you.

The Father tells his sons that starting points in life affect the whole journey. That's why Proverbs begins with, "The fear of the LORD is the beginning of knowledge; fools despise wisdom and instruction" (Proverbs 1:7). Proverbs was written so that we would gain more than just knowledge. Wisdom is knowledge skillfully applied in the right situations at the right time. We need the knowledge, but also we need God's instruction to apply that knowledge in a way that brings his blessing in his world. That is wisdom. Proverbs uses the relational father-son style common of Wisdom Literature of the Old Testament era and we're promised that the simple or naïve will gain real life, real-time help. Godly principles applied from the start of our lives set the trajectory toward successful living as God defines it.

How does our heavenly Father define successful living? It turns out that it is quite different from how the world defines it. Here are some ways Proverbs points us to living out "the fear of the LORD" in everyday life:

- Ask for wisdom before you think you need it (1:20–33).
- Do everything (even the smallest things) with honesty and integrity (11:1; cf 11:3, 6).

- Avoid sexual temptation at all costs. It will wreck havoc in your life (Proverbs 2:15–22; 5:1–23; 6:24–35; 7:1–27; 9:13–18; 22:14; 23:26–28).
- Work hard; don't be lazy (6:6–11).
- Learn self-control (4:20–27).
- Treat the poor and weak with compassion (14:31; 17:5).

Proverbs is the Father showing his sons how to live every day. Let him speak into your life every day!

Wisdom about People

Not only does the wisdom from Proverbs give us a map for decision-making, it also helps us understand people. A good father prepares his kids for what they will encounter in the real world because the people we meet will have great influence on our lives. So get to know the main types of people you'll meet in Proverbs and in the world—the simple, the fool (also called the scoffer), and the wise person.

> Wisdom cries aloud in the street, in the markets she raises her voice; at the head of the noisy streets she cries out; at the entrance of the city gates she speaks: "How long, O simple ones, will you love being simple? How long will scoffers delight in their scoffing and fools hate knowledge?" (Proverbs 1:20–22)

The proverbs of Solomon. A wise son makes a glad father, but a foolish son is a sorrow to his mother. (Proverbs 10:1)

According to Proverbs all the people you meet will fall into these three categories: the simple, the fool, and the wise. Helping you become a wise man is really the goal of the instruction in Proverbs. The wise man doesn't need to learn from his foolish mistakes. Instead he fears (honor/respects) his heavenly Father. Because he respects his Father, the wise man listens to his Father who is the source of all wisdom. In Proverbs the wise man is also called righteous, upright, diligent, understanding, and prudent.

From a New Testament perspective the wise man is redeemed by the cross of Christ and wants to live out of that new and abundant relationship with the Father. He *wants* to live his faith. He knows that salvation is for eternity, but the wise man also knows that salvation consists of knowing God and his ways starting *now* (John 17:3).

The wise son learns from our Father and this brings blessing to his life. He learns and keeps learning that doing life God's way is supremely better than his way or the way of the world. He knows that God isn't out to ruin his life. The wise man is the hero of the book of Proverbs. Wisdom enables men to wipe away the external clutter of a fallen world and live with clarity. The wise man is also the kind of men other men want to follow.

The *fool* is the anti-hero of Proverbs; he is the polar opposite of the wise man. The fool is the man who steadily and persistently resists God's grace for salvation and life: "Fools despise wisdom and instruction" (Proverbs 1:7b*)*. Fools are self-reliant and hostile to God's ways. In Proverbs the fool is also identified as wicked, lazy, and lacking sense. This hard-hearted spiritual condition means the fool will inevitably act in opposition to God's good ways. A man can be quite intelligent and still a fool. You can be brilliant and successful and still be a fool. If your heart is set in opposition to God, your moral and relational decisions will inevitably lead to a broken life.

We all do foolish things, but the fool never turns from his foolishness toward Christ. He doesn't ask for forgiveness and help. Sadly, as a pastor, I have met one man after another who fits the definition of a fool—they are successful in life, they have lots of nice things, but they lose their marriage and their children barely know them. Proverbs says fools resist forgiveness (Proverbs 14:9; 15:8), are a dangerous influence (Proverbs 13:20; 17:12), cause grief to their parents (Proverbs 10:1), but are not beyond hope (Proverbs 8:5).

The fool is the person who lives for today and doesn't want to accept that his actions will affect his future—his relationships, his health, his opportunities (Proverbs 6:1–5). I have talked with many men who didn't want to accept that their foolish ways will have long-term consequences. There was the man who didn't care to control his temper around his wife. Eventually she left him.

Another who thought his constant use of pornography wouldn't affect his marriage—it's now ended. There was the friend who didn't spend any time with his children when they were young—now he barely knows them. Another who chose to go along with a shady scheme for making money—now he is bankrupt and owes thousands to the government. And even sadder, my friend with lung disease who still isn't able to stop smoking. I share these stories to point out that sometimes we just don't want to stop doing life-destroying, foolish things, until it's nearly too late in the game.

But remember, even if you see areas of foolishness in your life, with God as your Father there is always hope. The fear of the Lord is the beginning of wisdom, and whether you are old or young, it's never too late to turn to your heavenly Father and ask for forgiveness for Jesus's sake. You *will* be forgiven. And God will redeem your foolishness. He has done it for me, and he will do it for you!

The last category, the simple man, is naïve, untaught, and unlearned in the ways of life as God defines life. In Proverbs the simple is called to get on the journey toward wisdom and stay there until wisdom characterizes him, rather than naivete. Proverbs says, "The simple believes everything, but the prudent [wise] gives thought to his steps" (Proverbs 14:15). You don't have to be young to be someone who has never given "thought to his steps." We can grow old and never grow up. I've met dozens of older men who are still immature in the way they think about God, people, and life.

I'll never forget a conversation I had with an older man and his wife. He said something hurtful to his wife right in front of me. His wife turned to me and said, "Do you see what I mean? He says things like that all the time." Turning to the man I said, "Why did you say that?" He was caught, but still replied, "What do you think I said?" When I repeated it back to him, he said "No way did I say that!" and then asserted over and over that he was innocent of being unkind. It would have been so much better for him to have just admitted it and apologized, but he didn't see how God's grace for him could give him the confidence to admit he was wrong. Although he was older, he was still "simple," a man who was not willing to become a student of God's love and to understand how that love could change his daily interactions with his wife.

The Lifelong Pursuit of Wisdom

I love what Wes Yoder says about our journey as men: "We are all sons, but we are called to be fathers, as, Henri Nouwen says, and, at the end of our days, patriarch."[1] If we pursue wisdom all of our lives, we will become patriarchs, resources for our families, churches, and communities. Becoming a wise man is a life-long pursuit surrounded and fueled by the grace of God that is there for the asking (James 1:5). Our Father is all-wise, and he is going to build wisdom into his sons. Like Father, like son.

Take It to Heart

1. What is God's definition of wisdom (Proverbs 1:7)? How important was wisdom to you growing up? What is the difference between knowledge and wisdom?

2. What did you learn about the wisdom given in Proverbs from this chapter? Are there times in your life when you have been "simple"? A "fool"? What were the consequences?

3. How does wisdom prevent us from foolishly damaging our own lives (Proverbs 1:20–33; 2:16–22; 5:1–23; 15:31)?

4. How can God's wisdom from Proverbs be applied to your work in business, ministry, the arts, education, government service, the military, etc.? Discuss how God's wisdom can impact your particular areas of employment.

5. Imagine how your church would benefit if the men of the church were all involved in the pursuit of wisdom as described in Proverbs. How would it affect your leadership team and decision making as a church? What long-term impact might it make in your church if the Father's sons were increasing in wisdom on a weekly basis?

6. How does the character of church leaders and godly men go hand in hand with biblical wisdom as taught in Proverbs (see 1 Timothy 3; Titus 1)?

10

The Grace-Giving Father

"Nothing fosters courage like a clear grasp of grace.
And nothing fosters fear like an ignorance of mercy."[1]
Max Lucado

Once there was a Spanish father and son (José) who, like many fathers and sons, had an angry argument where they both said hurtful things. The son stormed out saying he never wanted to see his father again, and the father said much the same. Then, as Ray Stedman tells the story,

> Years passed. The father regretted the things he had said in that moment of intense emotion. He longed for his son. Finally, the pain of separation became too much for him to bear. He left home and went searching across the length and breadth of Spain—but his son seemed to have disappeared without a trace.
>
> Finally, arriving in the capital city of Madrid, he went to a newspaper office and took out a personal ad in the classified section.

It read, "My son, José—I am sorry for the pain I've caused you. Please forgive me. I have forgiven you. I've looked everywhere for you and want only to see you again. I will be at the plaza fountain every day this week at noon. Please meet me there. Your father." It is said that hundreds of young men named José came to the plaza fountain that week, hoping to reestablish a relationship with their fathers.[2]

I get choked up when I read that story. Father-son relationships can be complex, hurtful, and lead to separation. Sons long to be close to their fathers, but as they grow up and have conflict with their dads, they often don't know how to get close to them. Often their dads—who should be able to take the lead in moving toward their son—have no idea how to do that, so fathers and sons remain tragically separated. In the many broken father-son stories I have heard over the years, unfortunately there are few stories like this example, where a father sees the light and "the pain of separation" from their sons becomes "too much for them to bear" and out of a "deep inability to do nothing" they search out their sons and do whatever is possible to reestablish ties.[3]

But we have a different father-son story, don't we? The very best father-son story is in the Bible. It's about a perfect Father and his imperfect sons (and daughters) who went astray. Our perfect heavenly Father, whose nature is loving, merciful, and gracious, comes after his sons at great cost to himself, to bring them home. It's the story of grace.

God's Grace Story

You can find the thread of God's grace through every story about God and his people in the Bible. There is no difference between the God of the Old Testament and the God of the New Testament. God has always been gracious to his people because that is his nature. Here's how God describes himself to Moses: "The LORD passed before him and proclaimed, 'The LORD, the LORD, a God merciful and gracious, slow to anger, and abounding in steadfast love and faithfulness" (Exodus 34:6).

Without grace we are lost, and with it we find new life and forgiveness and hope. Grace is God's *unearned favor* that he pours out when, where, and on whom he is pleased to be generous. The pinnacle of God's grace is seen in sending his Son, Jesus. It was because of grace that God the Father gave his Son for the sins of his people. It was God's grace that the Son freely gave himself for his enemies (Romans 5:6–8). And because of God's grace we are given the Spirit to give us the power to follow Jesus (2 Timothy 1:7).

The Greek word for grace, *charis,* is found over 120 times in the New Testament. Paul sums up what God's grace means to those who trust Jesus when he says, "For by grace you have been saved through faith. And this is not your own doing; it is the gift of God, not a result of works, so that no one may boast" (Ephesians 2:8–9).

God's Grace for You

Religion is trying to get God to accept us by what we do to please him. But being a Christian is not about religion. The only way to be acceptable to God is by faith in Christ alone.

Paul reminds us that before Christ meets us we're "dead in the trespasses and sins" of open rebellion and resistance to God (Ephesians 2:1). He graphically describes the true nature of our sin by saying, "We all once lived in the passions of our flesh, carrying out the desires of the body and the mind" (2:3). That's so true! Before we came to Christ we simply went along with our passions and let them guide us in our behavior. We hurt others and ourselves, revealing that we really were not alive to God's way at all. To be dead, spiritually dead to God, means that we have no relationship with him and no interest in or ability to move toward him. Dead men have just one hope—the grace of God that makes them alive in Christ.

God shows us his mercy and great love (2:4) in withholding his judgment for our sin and in giving us the gift of faith, the grace of faith in Jesus Christ as Savior and Lord. This unearned and unrequested favor of God is the power that enables us to see our sin, come to the end of what we can do for ourselves, and see our own brokenness and emptiness. It's only then that we put our trust in Jesus Christ as God's substitute for us on the cross.

We are the sons who went away from a perfect Father. He comes in search of us by sacrificing his own Son, Jesus, and calling us home. We are the sons who didn't think we were the problem, but by grace have come to see that we are wrong, not God. We are the sons who now have nothing in our hands or hearts to give God. We only have our sin and shame to offer God. Yet Jesus's death on the cross paid for our sins as a free gift from our heavenly Father, "For by grace you have been saved through faith. And this is not of your own doing; it is the gift of God" (Ephesians 2:8).

Grace is what we desperately need for salvation, but also what we need for every day of our lives. Because even though we're forgiven for our sins once and for all, we sin daily—we lose sight of the importance of others, we run after all kinds of God replacements (idols), and we forget our high status as sons of God through faith in Christ. Every day we need the Father's grace for forgiveness and help. It's so easy for us as men to try to do life on our own, without our Father. But self-made men inevitably self-destruct. Without God's grace, we won't survive. We need to come back to the Father through Jesus every single morning, noon, and night.

A Grace Manifesto

Paul, in the book of Romans, fills our minds and hearts with how God's grace changes needy sinners. All have sinned, but

- By grace we are freely justified (Romans 3:23–24).
- Because we are justified we have peace with God (Romans 5:1).
- Because of God's grace those who are in Christ are no longer condemned (Romans 8:10).
- Because of God's grace all things work together for the good of those who love God (Romans 8:28).
- And because of God's grace in Jesus nothing can separate us from the love of God (Romans 8:35–38).

God's grace is the source for everything Jesus has done for us and everything good that has happened in us. There's no such thing as bad luck or good luck for a Christ-following man. By grace we belong to our heavenly Father, by grace we are called his sons, and because of his grace all of life's events are tied to his good purpose for us. It all started before we were born as God *foreknew* (foreloved) us and in love *predestined* (predetermined) us to be so radically transformed as men that we would take on the same character as Jesus, and that Jesus would be the first of many sons to follow (Romans 8:29–30).

Grace is free to us for the asking, but oh-so-costly for our Savior. We couldn't be called into a relationship with

God and justified until the work of atonement was accomplished on the cross. But Jesus was the faithful Son, the lion who became a lamb as our substitute in keeping the law perfectly and receiving our curse completely, so that we could be justified (declared not guilty) from our sins. This work of Christ is so thorough, so complete, so effective, that Paul tells us that because we're united to Jesus through faith we are in fact *glorified* already.

As a man following Christ there is simply nothing more to be accomplished for us or that we can accomplish for ourselves (Romans 8:31–38). Jesus is completely sufficient.

What Do You Do with Grace?

Receive grace. Paul's letters start and end with the exhortation to receive grace because we need grace for salvation and then minute by minute for everything else as Christ followers. When a man is constantly nourished by the unconditional love and acceptance of God through Christ, God's power surges into his soul and he develops a muscular Christianity that faces challenges and trials by faith. Impotence is frustrating. Knowing God's grace for you—his acceptance for you in Christ—builds backbone, dispels fears, and overcomes evil. As you ask for grace to face your day, the Spirit of God works in your life so you can live as a welcomed-home son of God.

Renew your identity in grace. Grace is not just for the first time we come to Christ in faith. We need to renew

145

our identity in grace every day and even multiple times during the day. The apostle Paul in Galatians scolds the church for "deserting him who called you in the grace of Christ and . . . turning to a different gospel" (Galatians 1:6).

Why was Paul so adamant about the gospel of grace? When a man turns away from the gospel of grace he's turning back to the exhausting treadmill of building his own identity. By God's grace you are a son. Don't turn away from your sonship! Everything you truly need in life is bound up in your relationship with your heavenly Father. Paul didn't want the Galatians to go back to a futile, enslaving way of life. Instead he wanted them to remember and step into their adoption as sons of the living God (Galatians 4:3–7).

What does renewing my identity in grace look like? The other day I woke up in the middle of the night. Feelings of competitiveness, ineffectiveness, failure, and unworthiness laced with anxiety woke me and kept me up. I prayed, *Father, I need grace, right now.* I still couldn't go back to sleep, so instead of tossing in bed, I went running. While I ran, I listened to the Father who likes to speak to me when I'm pounding the pavement. He reminded me that I'm not what I thought I was, but that I am less, and a whole lot more. On my own I'm less impressive than I think I am. Yet, in Christ, I am God's beloved son, forever. My identity as his son is separated from my work and the roles I hold.

When self-absorbed anxiety fills my mind and I try to find status in approval or performance (which doesn't just happen at night but throughout the day), I can stop, remember it's all of grace, and ask the Spirit to knock that twisted thinking out of me. Sometimes I stop for a minute and say, "Father, forgive me for looking everywhere but you for approval and a sense of who I am. You're my Abba, and Jesus you made that possible. Thank you that your grace is so powerful that you can bring me back to sanity with it! Now, please help me live in grace today." Renew your identity in grace and, like me, repent when you start moving away from grace to find status in position, power, sex, approval, and performance.

Remember grace. Because it's so easy to forget who we are in Christ and what he has done for us, we need to constantly remember how God has changed us *by grace*. If it weren't for grace you and I would still be spinning our wheels, disconnected from the Father, and going nowhere in particular. All that has changed now. Grace is a historical reality in our lives that has unique power when a man consciously remembers and rehearses how God brought it to his life. The great apostle Paul never forgot who he was before he met Jesus.

> The saying is trustworthy and deserving of full acceptance, that Christ Jesus came into the world to save sinners, of whom I am the foremost. But I received mercy for this reason,

> that in me, as the foremost, Jesus Christ might
> display his perfect patience as an example to
> those who were to believe in him for eternal
> life. To the King of ages, immortal, invisible,
> the only God, be honor and glory forever and
> ever. Amen. (1 Timothy 1:15–17)

When we remember where we were and then what God has done for us in Jesus, we are filled with joy that leads naturally to worship. There are many days, even Sundays before church, when I don't feel like God is all that great and exciting, but I *know* that feelings shouldn't dominate me. Getting back to worship is as simple as recalling that grace we have been given. Then, like Paul, we can overflow with worship for the King of ages.

Remain in grace. I'm always tempted to move on from grace, but there really is no other rock solid foundation for life. Grace is our only firm footing. Jesus tells us this when he says, "As the Father has loved me, so have I loved you. Abide in my love" (John 15:9). When we stay close to Jesus, we find rest, rejuvenation, and power for living. Well-loved people are the most energetic and sacrificial people you'll ever meet. They give so generously because they are drawing from a deep and continuously replenished reservoir of power.

We must get *immediate grace* because when we sin we feel *immediate* guilt. Without immediately remembering that because of God's grace in Christ we are forgiven, we will try to handle guilt on our own. That means either denying our guilt or trying to atone for it ourselves. It's easy to think that being a Christian means trying harder to do better. But the frantic work of trying to save ourselves is not the way of grace. It's back to slavery. What some call legalism or moralism is a tyrant that continues to demand more and more, and yet you can never do enough.

Instead, when you sin, reflect, ask *Why did I do that? What can I learn?* Then, confess your sin, agree with God, and repent, but quickly receive the Father's forgiveness for Jesus's sake. Then dance (if you do that), and get going again. Every time we sin we have an opportunity to renounce salvation by anything except grace through faith (Ephesians 2:8) and to be humbly thankful for a Father who loves so thoroughly. Because of the cross, the Father is always willing to give *immediate grace* to us when we ask for it. But we have to ask! When you see your sin for what it is and go to Jesus, don't waste time in guilt or trying harder. Instead, move toward true service. We have to remain in grace. Without God's grace we have nothing.

Douglas Coupland says it so well, "My secret is that I need God—that I am sick and can no longer make it alone. I need God to help me give, because I no longer seem to be capable of giving; to help me be kind, as I no longer seem capable of kindness; to help me love, as I seem beyond being able to love."[4]

Knowing God's grace takes the paranoia about sinning away. The truth is I will sin and so will you. Grace says you and I don't have to wear masks and pretend to be what we aren't. When we sin, we can say so and move on. You and I can afford to be honest about our sins, because we are saved by grace.

Grace is so powerful that when you remain in it, you're released from being the Messiah for everyone around you. There are issues in you, in your family, in your friends, in your coworkers, and certainly in others in the country that you cannot fix. Grace frees you from the depression that comes from living in a messed-up world, and causes you to engage the world where you can without the obsessive and impossible need to fix everything.

Reveal grace. A friend of mine once said, "Those who teach grace ought to be gracious." When you deeply drink of grace, it ought to pervade your relationships. Grace really does affect everything about us. Just as the Father understands that I was a slave to sin before he met me and graciously made me his son, I need to understand that people struggle with their own sin and be gracious to them as fellow sinners. People have bad days—it's a broken world, after all. Grace has helped me accept that my wife, kids, friends, and all others around me have bad days too, where their sins are on display just like mine. Realizing this has allowed me to let go of people's "digs," sarcasm, or comments about me, and even agree with their direct comments about my weaknesses. It's so freeing to say, "Yep, that's me alright. You put your finger right on it!" without defending myself.

Grace is such a powerful force that it reminds me to forgive as I have been forgiven. Instead of holding myself and others to a high (and impossible standard), God's grace reminds me that we are all weak and need daily help. Grace produces humble men who can acknowledge their own weaknesses. Can you imagine our impact on the world with the gospel of Jesus Christ when—as hard-boiled and task-oriented as we can be—we reveal grace to others around us? A grace-permeated man commands notice.

Those who get grace become natural evangelists. Those who were once captives to sin and are now freed by God's grace in Christ get quite talkative. Now they have something and Someone to talk about. Dorothy Day, the founder of the Catholic Worker Movement, had a simple motto, "It's all grace." The former Catholic priest Brennan Manning titled his last book *All Is Grace*.

The gospel of grace changes everything and impacts everything in a man's life and relationships, including what and who he talks about, and how he talks about it all. As Christians how should we relate to the world around us that so often disagrees with us? What Richard Mouw said in his book *Uncommon Decency* is surely true: "Without grace, civility cannot endure. And what else but grace could possibly sustain us in those moments when we have no choice but to move beyond civility?"[5] Grace leads us to be assertive, but not controlling. We can relax because we've left control to the One who actually does control. His shoes are too big for us to fill anyway.

Grace and Glory

How incredible it is to be a man graced by the Father! Grace makes a man everything he really wants to be, as well as the man others around him most need. God's grace in Christ makes a man who is a one hundred percent a sinner into one who is one hundred percent forgiven and worthy. We're sons, not sinless. Because we're graced, we're still growing, and we are an ongoing force to be reckoned with in a world that needs Jesus.

Grace grows in us the longer it is consciously cultivated in our lives. The more we focus on God's unearned favor in Jesus, the more we will find it creeping into every area of our lives and freeing us more and more. The Father brings his glory into the lives of his sons when he unleashes grace. Let the glory flow!

Grace makes a man a bondservant through whom God's glory flows. As H. C. G. Moule says,

> To be a bondservant is terrible in the abstract. To be Jesus Christ's bondservant is paradise in the concrete. Self-surrender, taken alone, is a plunge into a cold void. When it is surrender to "the Son of God, who loved me and gave himself for me" (Galatians 2:20) it is the bright home-coming of the soul to the sphere of life and power.[6]

Brothers, may the grace of God assure you that because of Jesus and Jesus alone you are beloved sons. And may that assurance allow his glory to free you to live large. May your complete reliance on Jesus drive the religious crazy, give hope to the broken, and fill you with deep joy. May the Father's grace make you a man of grace. Like Father, like son.

Take It to Heart

1. How would you define and explain God's grace if asked? What's a good grace "elevator" speech (Ephesians 2:1–10)?

2. How does God's grace to us go against a man's natural tendency to put his confidence in what he has accomplished (Philippians 3:1–8)?

3. What does God's grace do to a man's identity? Why is grace so important to us as we daily follow Christ as the Father's sons (Galatians 4:3–7)?

4. What does God's grace mean to you personally, and how does it transform you?

5. How can you learn to live in grace (i.e., to allow the grace of God to permeate your Christian life as his son)? Are there some men you know who need and want to be on a similar journey of being "graced" day in and day out? How could you encourage each other to live in grace?

6. As a challenge, read one of Paul's letters (Galatians, Ephesians, Philippians, or Colossians, for example) from start to finish in one sitting. Circle the word "grace" throughout. Describe how grace as a theme affects everything Paul is writing about. How do you think grace changes everything in a Christian's life?

7. Ask the Spirit to teach you to be the kind of Christ-follower who daily receives and is shaped by grace from his Father.

Endnotes

Chapter 1

1. David Katz, ed., *Fathers and Sons, 11 Great Writers Talk about Their Dads, Their Boys, and What It Means to Be a Man* (New York: Esquire Books (Hearst), 2010), 59.

2. John Eldredge, *Wild at Heart, Discovering the Secret of a Man's Soul* (Nashville: Thomas Nelson, 2001), 59.

3. Thomas Moore, *Care of the Soul, A Guide for Cultivating Depth and Sacredness in Everyday Life* (New York: Harper Collins, 1992), 34.

4. Ditta M. Oliker, "The Long Reach of Childhood, How Early Experiences Shape You Forever," *Psychology Today* 6 (2011).

5. David Popenoe, *Life without Father: Compelling New Evidence That Fatherhood and Marriage Are Indispensable for the Good of Children and Society* (New York: The Free Press, 1996), 163.

Chapter 2

1. Steve Brown, *If God Is in Charge: Thoughts on the Nature of God for Skeptics, Christians, and Skeptical Christians* (Nashville: Thomas Nelson, 1983), 13.

2. Story used by permission.
3. A. W. Tozer, *The Knowledge of the Holy* (New York: Harper and Row, 1961), 9.
4. J. I. Packer, *Knowing God* (Downers Grove: Intervarsity Press, 1973).

Chapter 3

1. http://www.brainyquote.com/quotes/quotes/v/victorhugo152556.html.
2. Russell Moore, "W.W. Jay-Z?", *Christianity Today*, May 10, 2013, 27.
3. R. Albert Mohler Jr., *From Boy to Man, The Marks of Manhood* (Louisville: The Southern Baptist Theological Seminary, 2010), 8–9.

Chapter 4

1. Brennan Manning, *The Ragamuffin Gospel* (Sisters, Oregon: Multnomah Books, 1990), 25.
2. David D. Gilmore, *Manhood in the Making: Cultural Concepts of Masculinity* (New Haven: Yale University Press, 1990), 143.
3. Ibid., 144–45.
4. Ibid., 9.
5. Michael Herzfeld, *The Poetics of Manhood: Contest and Identity in a Cretan Mountain Village* (Princeton: Princeton University Press, 1985), 17, quoted in David D. Gilmore, *Manhood in the Making: Cultural Concepts of Masculinity* (New Haven: Yale University Press, 1990), 30.
6. http://www.historynet.com/abraham-lincoln-quotes.

7. Stephen E. Ambrose, *Crazy Horse and Custer: The Parallel Lives of Two American Warriors* (New York: Doubleday & Company, 1975), xv.

8. Timothy Keller, *Every Good Endeavor: Connecting Your Work to God's Work* (New York: Dutton, 2012), 21, 23.

9. David Blankenhorn, *Fatherless America: Confronting Our Most Urgent Social Problem* (New York: Harper Perennial, 1996), 1.

Chapter 5

1. Thomas Merton, *New Seeds of Contemplation* (The Abbey of Gethsemani, 1961), 295.

2. Chris Mannix, "A Father's Faith," *Sports Illustrated*, September 9, 2013, 53–55.

3. Elisabeth Elliot, *The Mark of a Man* (New Jersey: Revell Company, 1981), 164.

4. Rudolph W. Giuliani, *Leadership* (New York: Hyperion Books, 2002), 48.

5. Michael Horton, *The Christian Faith: A Systematic Theology for Pilgrims on the Way* (Grand Rapids: Zondervan, 2011), 408, 411; John M. Frame, *Systematic Theology: An Introduction to Christian Belief* (New Jersey: P & R Publishing, 2013), 66; R. C. Sproul, *Truths We Confess: A Layman's Guide to the Westminster Confession of Faith*, Vol. One, *The Triune God* (New Jersey: P & R Publishing, 2006), 183; Wayne Grudem, *Systematic Theology: An Introduction to Biblical Doctrine* (Grand Rapids: Zondervan, 1994), 463.

6. Anthony Campolo, Jr., *The Power Delusion* (Wheaton: Victor Books, 1984), 9.

7. Larry Crabb, *Men and Women: Enjoying the Difference* (Grand Rapids: Zondervan, 1991), 157.

8. Ibid.

9. Ibid.

10. Richard D. Phillips, *The Masculine Mandate: God's Calling to Men* (Orlando: Reformation Trust, 2010), 14–15.

11. Bruce K. Waltke, *Genesis: A Commentary* (Grand Rapids: Zondervan, 2001), 85.

Chapter 6

1. Martin Luther, *Commentary on Galatians: Modern-English Edition* (Grand Rapids: Fleming H. Revell, 1988), 315.

2. Ibid., 317.

3. Ibid., 314.

4. Ted Olsen, "If You See Something, Say Something," *Christianity Today*, May 2015, 2.

5. François Fenelon, *Let Go* (Pennsylvania: Whitaker House, 1973), 64–65.

6. Elisabeth Elliot, *Through Gates of Splendor* (Wheaton: Tyndale House, 2005).

Chapter 7

1. Jon Krakauer, *Into the Wild* (New York: Random House, 1996), 57.

2. Helen Keller, The Quotations Page, http://www.quotationspage.com/quotes/Helen_Keller.

3. Candice Millard, *The River of Doubt: Theodore Roosevelt's Darkest Journey* (New York: Broadway Books, 2006), 262.

4. Ibid., 252.

5. Ibid., 267.

6. William Hendriksen, *New Testament Commentary: Exposition of the Gospel According to Matthew* (Michigan: Baker, 1973), 251.

7. Eric Metaxas, *Bonhoeffer: Pastor, Martyr, Prophet, Spy* (Nashville: Thomas Nelson, 2010), 528.

8. Erwin Raphael McManus, *The Barbarian Way* (Nashville: Thomas Nelson, 2005), 107.

9. Andrew Murray, *Abide in Christ* (Connecticut: Keats Publishing, 1973), 1–2.

Chapter 8

1. Stephen W. Brown, *Welcome to the Family* (New Jersey: Fleming H. Revell Co., 1990), 86.

2. Steve Brown, *Approaching God: How to Pray* (Nashville: Moorings, 1996), ix.

3. David Wilkie, *Coffee with Jesus* (Downers Grove: Intervarsity, 2013), 61.

4. Richard J. Mouw, *Uncommon Decency: Christian Civility in an Uncivil World* (Downers Grove: Intervarsity, 2010), 173.

Chapter 9

1. Wes Yoder, *Bond of Brothers: Connecting with Other Men Beyond Work, Weather, and Sports* (Grand Rapids: Zondervan, 2010), 68.

Chapter 10

1. Max Lucado, *Fearless: Imagine Your Life Without Fear* (Nashville: Thomas Nelson, 2009), 38.

2. Ray C. Stedman, *Talking with My Father: Jesus Teaches on Prayer* (Grand Rapids: Discovery House, 1997), 19.

3. Mark Batterson, *All In: You Are One Decision Away from a Totally Different Life* (Grand Rapids: Zondervan, 2013), 35.

4. Douglas Coupland, https://www.goodreads.com/author/quotes/1886.Douglas_Coupland.

5. Mouw, *Uncommon Decency*, 147.

6. Handley C. G. Moule, *The Epistle of St. Paul to the Romans* (Cincinnati: Jennings & Graham, 1893), 11.

Are you tired of
"do more, try harder" religion?

Key Life has only one message, to communicate the radical grace of God to sinners and sufferers. Because of what Jesus has done, God's not mad at you.

On radio, in print, on CDs and online, we're proclaiming the scandalous reality of Jesus' good news of radical grace...leading to radical freedom, infectious joy and surprising faithfulness to Christ.

For all things grace, visit us at **KeyLife.org**